# RESUMES
## FOR
# BANKING
## AND
# FINANCIAL
# CAREERS

**VGM** Professional Resumes Series

# RESUMES
## FOR
## BANKING
## AND
## FINANCIAL
## CAREERS

The Editors of
VGM Career Books

Second Edition, With Sample Cover Letters

*VGM Career Books*

Chicago   New York   San Francisco   Lisbon   London   Madrid   Mexico City
Milan   New Delhi   San Juan   Seoul   Singapore   Sydney   Toronto

**Library of Congress Cataloging-in-Publication Data**

Resumes for banking and financial careers / the editors of VGM Career Books. — 2nd ed.
    p.    cm. — (VGM professional resumes series)
        ISBN 0-658-01103-0
        1. Resumes (Employment).    2. Cover letters.    3. Banks and banking—Vocational
guidance.    4. Financial services industry—Vocational guidance.    5. College
graduates—Employment.    I. VGM Career Books (Firm)    II. Series

    HF5383 .R433    2001
    808'.06665—dc21                                                      00-53367

*We would like to acknowledge the assistance of Luisa Gerasimo
in the compiling and editing of this book.*

## VGM Career Books
### A Division of The McGraw·Hill Companies

    2 3 4 5  6 7 8 9 0 VLP VLP 0 5 4 3 2 1


ISBN 0-658-01103-0

This book was set in Minion by City Desktop Productions
Printed and bound by Vicks Lithograph

McGraw-Hill books are available at special quantity discounts to use as premiums and
sales promotions, or for use in corporate training programs. For more information, please
write to the Director of Special Sales, Professional Publishing, McGraw-Hill, Two Penn
Plaza, New York, NY 10121-2298. Or contact your local bookstore.

This book is printed on acid-free paper.

# Contents

# RESUMES
## FOR
# BANKING
## AND
# FINANCIAL
# CAREERS

# Introduction

Your resume is the first impression you give a prospective employer. Though you may be articulate, intelligent, and charming in person, a poor resume may prevent you from ever having the opportunity to demonstrate your interpersonal skills, because it may prevent you from being called for an interview. While few people have ever been hired solely on the basis of their resume, a well-written, well-organized resume can go a long way toward helping you land an interview. Your resume's main purpose is to get you that interview. The rest is up to you and the employer. If you both feel that you are right for the job and the job is right for you, chances are you will be hired.

A resume must catch the reader's attention yet still be easy to read and to the point. Resume styles have changed over the years. Today, brief and focused resumes are preferred. Employers no longer have the patience, or the time, to review several pages of solid type. A resume should be only one page long, if possible, and never more than two pages. Time is a precious commodity in today's business world; the resume that is concise and straightforward will usually be the one that gets noticed.

Let's not make the mistake, though, of assuming that writing a brief resume means that you can take less care in preparing it. A successful resume takes time and thought, but if you are willing to make the effort, the rewards are well worth it. Think of your resume as a sales brochure with the product being you. You want to sell yourself to a prospective employer. This book is designed to help you prepare a resume that will further your career—to land that next job, or first job, or to return to the workforce after years of absence. So, read on. Make the effort and then reap the rewards that a strong resume can bring to your career. Let's get to it!

# The Elements of a Good Resume

A winning resume is made from the elements that employers are most interested in seeing when reviewing a job applicant. These basic elements are the key ingredients of a successful resume and become the section headings of your resume. The following is a list of elements that may be used in a resume. Some are essential, some are optional. We will be discussing these in this chapter to give you a better understanding of each element's role in the makeup of your resume:

1. Heading

2. Objective

3. Work Experience

4. Education

5. Honors

6. Activities

7. Certificates and Licenses

8. Professional Memberships

9. Special Skills

10. Personal Information

11. References

The first step in preparing your resume is to gather information about yourself and your past accomplishments. Later you will refine this information, rewrite it in the most effective language, and organize it into an attractive layout. First, let's take a look at each of these important elements individually.

## Heading

The heading may seem to be a simple enough element in your resume, but be careful not to take it lightly. The heading should be placed at the top of your resume and should include your name, home address, and telephone numbers. If you can take calls at your current place of business, include your business number, since most employers will attempt to contact you during the business day. If this is not possible, purchase an answering machine that allows you to retrieve your messages while you are away from home. This way you can make sure you don't miss important phone calls. *Always* include your phone number on your resume. It is crucial that prospective employers are able to have immediate contact with you when they need to.

## Objective

When seeking a particular career path, it is important to list a job objective on your resume. This statement helps employers determine the direction that you see yourself heading, so that they can determine whether your goals are in line with the position available. The objective is normally one sentence long and describes your employment goals clearly and concisely. See the sample resumes in this book for examples of objective statements.

The job objective will vary depending on your personality, your career field, and your goals. It can be either specific or general, but it should always be to the point.

In some cases, this element is not necessary, but it is usually a good idea to include your objective. It gives your potential employer an idea of where you are coming from and where you want to go.

The objective statement is better left out, however, if you are uncertain of the exact title of the job you seek. In such a case, the inclusion of an overly specific objective statement could result in your not being considered for a variety of acceptable positions; incorporate your job objective into your cover letter instead.

## Work Experience

Work experience is arguably the most important element of them all. It will provide the central focus of your resume, so it is necessary that this section be as complete as possible. Only by examining your work experience in depth can you get to the heart of your accomplishments and present them in a way that demonstrates the strength of your qualifications. Of course, someone just out of school will have less work experience than someone who has been working for a number of years, but the amount of information isn't the most important thing—how it is presented, and how it highlights you as a person and as a worker will be what counts most.

As you work on this section of your resume, be aware of the need for accuracy. Include all necessary information about each of your jobs, including job title, dates, employer, city, state, responsibilities, special projects, and accomplishments. Be sure to list only company accomplishments for which you were directly responsible. If you haven't participated in any special projects, that's all right—this area may not be relevant to certain jobs.

The most common way to list your work experience is in *reverse chronological order*. In other words, start with your most recent job and work your way backward. This way your prospective employer sees your current (and often most important) job before seeing your past jobs. Your most recent position, if the most important, should also be the one that includes the most information as compared to your previous positions. If you are just out of school, show your summer employment and part-time work, though in this case your education will most likely be more important than your work experience.

The following worksheets will help you gather information about your past jobs.

## WORK EXPERIENCE

Job One:

Job Title _____

Dates _____

Employer _____

City, State _____

Major Duties _____

_____

_____

_____

_____

_____

_____

_____

_____

Special Projects _____

_____

_____

_____

Accomplishments _____

_____

_____

_____

_____

_____

_____

_____

**Job Two:**

Job Title _____

Dates _____

Employer _____

City, State _____

Major Duties _____

_____

_____

_____

_____

_____

_____

_____

Special Projects _____

_____

_____

_____

Accomplishments _____

_____

_____

_____

_____

_____

_____

_____

**Job Three:**

Job Title _____

Dates _____

Employer _____

City, State _____

Major Duties _____

_____

_____

_____

_____

_____

_____

_____

Special Projects _____

_____

_____

_____

Accomplishments _____

_____

_____

_____

_____

_____

_____

_____

**Job Four:**

Job Title _____

Dates _____

Employer _____

City, State _____

Major Duties _____

_____

_____

_____

_____

_____

_____

Special Projects _____

_____

_____

_____

Accomplishments _____

_____

_____

_____

_____

_____

_____

_____

## Education

Education is the second most important element of a resume. Your educational background is often a deciding factor in an employer's decision to hire you. Be sure to stress your accomplishments in school with the same finesse that you stressed your accomplishments at work. If you are looking for your first job, your education will be your greatest asset, since your work experience will most likely be minimal. In this case, the education section becomes the most important. You will want to include any degrees or certificates you received, your major area of concentration, any honors, and any relevant activities. List your most recent schooling first. If you have completed graduate-level work, begin with that and work in reverse chronological order through your undergraduate education. If you have completed an undergraduate degree, you may choose whether to list your high school experience or not. Do so only if your high school grade point average was well above average.

The following worksheets will help you gather information for this section of your resume. Also included are supplemental worksheets for honors and for activities. Sometimes honors and activities are listed in a section separate from education, most often near the end of the resume.

**EDUCATION**

School One _____

Major or Area of Concentration _____

Degree _____

Dates _____

School Two _____

Major or Area of Concentration _____

Degree _____

Dates _____

## Honors

In the honors section, list any awards, honors, or memberships in honorary societies that you have received. Usually these are of an academic nature, but you can also list any honor received for special achievement in sports, clubs, or other school activities. Always include the name of the organization honoring you and the date(s) received. Use the worksheet below to help gather your honors information.

### HONORS

Honor _____

Awarding Organization _____

Date(s) _____

Honor _____

Awarding Organization _____

Date(s) _____

Honor _____

Awarding Organization _____

Date(s) _____

Honor _____

Awarding Organization _____

Date(s) _____

## Activities

You may have been active in different organizations or clubs during your years at school; often an employer will look at such involvement as evidence of initiative and dedication. Your ability to take an active role, especially a leadership role, in a group should be included on your resume. Use the worksheet provided to list your activities and accomplishments in this area. In general, you should exclude any organization whose name indicates the race, creed, sex, age, marital status, sexual orientation, or nation of origin of its members.

## ACTIVITIES

Organization/Activity _____

Accomplishments _____

_____

_____

Organization/Activity _____

Accomplishments _____

_____

_____

Organization/Activity _____

Accomplishments _____

_____

_____

Organization/Activity _____

Accomplishments _____

_____

_____

As your work experience increases through the years, your school activities and honors will play less of a role in your resume, and eventually you will most likely list only your degree and any major honors you received. As time goes by, your job performance becomes the most important factor to a prospective employer. Your resume should change over the years to reflect this.

## Certificates and Licenses

If your chosen career path requires specialized training, you may already have certificates or licenses. You should list these if the job you are seeking requires them and you, of course, have acquired them. If you have applied for a license but have not yet received it, use the phrase "application pending."

License requirements vary by state. If you have moved or are planning to move to another state, check with that state's board or licensing agency for all licensing requirements.

Always be sure that all of the information you list is completely accurate. Locate copies of your certificates and licenses and check the exact date and name of the accrediting agency. Use the following worksheet to list your certificates and licenses.

### CERTIFICATES AND LICENSES

Name of License _____

Licensing Agency _____

Date Issued _____

Name of License _____

Licensing Agency _____

Date Issued _____

Name of License _____

Licensing Agency _____

Date Issued _____

## Professional Memberships

Another potential element in your resume is a section listing professional memberships. Use this section to list involvement in professional associations, unions, and similar organizations. It is to your advantage to list any professional memberships that pertain to the job you are seeking. Be sure to include the dates of your involvement and whether you took part in any special activities or held any offices within the organization. Use the following worksheet to gather your information.

### PROFESSIONAL MEMBERSHIPS

Name of Organization _____

Offices Held _____

Activities _____

Date(s) _____

Name of Organization _____

Offices Held _____

Activities _____

Date(s) _____

Name of Organization _____

Offices Held _____

Activities _____

Date(s) _____

Name of Organization _____

Offices Held _____

Activities _____

Date(s) _____

## Special Skills

The special skills section of your resume is the place to mention any abilities you have that could relate to the job you are seeking. This is the part of your resume where you have the opportunity to demonstrate certain talents and experiences that are not necessarily a part of your educational or work experience. Common examples include fluency in a foreign language or knowledge of a particular computer application.

Special skills can encompass a wide range of your talents—remember to list only skills that relate to the type of work you are looking for.

## Personal Information

Some people include personal information on their resumes. This is generally not recommended, but you might wish to include it if you think that something in your personal life, such as a hobby or talent, has some bearing on the position you are seeking. This type of information is often referred to at the beginning of an interview, when it is used as an "icebreaker." Of course, personal information regarding race, creed, sex, age, marital status, sexual orientation, or nation of origin should never appear on any resume.

## References

References are not usually listed on the resume, but a prospective employer needs to know that you have references who may be contacted if necessary. All that is necessary to include in your resume regarding references is a sentence at the bottom stating, "References are available upon request," in case a prospective employer requests a list of references. Check with whomever you list to see if it is all right for you to use them as a reference. Forewarn them that they may receive a call regarding a reference for you. This way they can be prepared to give you the best reference possible.

# *Writing Your Resume*

Now that you have gathered all of the information for each of the sections of your resume, it's time to write out each section in a way that will get the attention of whoever is reviewing it. The type of language you use in your resume will affect its success. Translate your information into a language that will cause a potential employer to take notice.

Resume writing is not like expository writing or creative writing. It embodies a functional, direct writing style and focuses on the use of action words. By using action words in your writing, you effectively stress past accomplishments. Action words demonstrate your initiative and highlight your talents. Writing with action words and strong verbs characterizes you to potential employers as an energetic, active person. Remember, your writing is all they know of you until you go in for the interview; your resume will be their first impression.

The following is a list of verbs commonly used in resume writing. Use this list to choose the action words that can help your resume become strong:

| | |
|---|---|
| administered | billed |
| advised | built |
| analyzed | carried out |
| arranged | channeled |
| assembled | collected |
| assumed responsibility | communicated |

compiled                          maintained

completed                         managed

conducted                         met with

contacted                         motivated

contracted                        negotiated

coordinated                       operated

counseled                         orchestrated

created                           ordered

cut                               organized

designed                          oversaw

determined                        performed

developed                         planned

directed                          prepared

dispatched                        presented

distributed                       produced

documented                        programmed

edited                            published

established                       purchased

expanded                          recommended

functioned as                     recorded

gathered                          reduced

handled                           referred

hired                             represented

implemented                       researched

improved                          reviewed

inspected                         saved

interviewed                       screened

introduced                        served as

invented                          served on

| sold | tested |
|------|--------|
| suggested | trained |
| supervised | typed |
| taught | wrote |

Now take a look at the information you put down on the work experience worksheets. Take that information and rewrite it in paragraph form, using verbs to highlight your actions and accomplishments. Let's look at two versions of an example, remembering that what matters here is the writing style, and not the particular job responsibilities given in our sample.

## WORK EXPERIENCE
### *Regional Sales Manager*

Manager of sales representatives from seven states. Responsible for twelve food chain accounts in the East. In charge of directing the sales force in planned selling toward specific goals. Supervisor and trainer of new sales representatives. Consulting for customers in the areas of inventory management and quality control.

*Special Projects*: Coordinator and sponsor of annual food industry sales seminar.

*Accomplishments*: Monthly regional volume went up twenty-five percent during my tenure while, at the same time, a proper sales/cost ratio was maintained. Customer-company relations improved significantly.

Below is the rewritten version of this information, using action words. Notice how much stronger it sounds.

## WORK EXPERIENCE
### *Regional Sales Manager*

Managed sales representatives from seven states. Handled twelve food chain accounts in the eastern United States. Directed the sales force in planned selling toward specific goals. Supervised and trained new sales representatives. Consulted for customers in the areas of inventory management and quality control. Coordinated and sponsored the annual Food Industry Seminar. Increased monthly regional volume twenty-five percent and helped to improve customer-company relations during my tenure.

Another way of constructing the work experience section is by using actual job descriptions. Job descriptions are rarely written using the proper resume language, but they do include all the information necessary to create this section of your resume. Take the description of one of the jobs you are including on your resume (if you have access to it), and turn it into an action-oriented paragraph. Below is an example of a job description followed by a version of the same description written using action words and actual job details. Again, pay attention to the style of writing, as the details of your own work experience will be unique.

## WORK EXPERIENCE
### *Public Administrator I*

*Responsibilities*: Coordinate and direct public services to meet the needs of the nation, state, or community. Analyze problems; work with special committees and public agencies; recommend solutions to governing bodies.

*Aptitudes and Skills*: Ability to relate to and communicate with people; solve complex problems through analysis; plan, organize, and implement policies and programs. Knowledge of political systems, financial management, personnel administration, program evaluation, and organizational theory.

## WORK EXPERIENCE
### *Public Administrator I*

Wrote pamphlets and conducted discussion groups to inform citizens of legislative processes and consumer issues. Organized and supervised twenty-five interviewers. Trained interviewers in effective communication skills.

Now that you have learned how to word your resume, you are ready for the next step in your quest for a winning resume: assembly and layout.

# Chapter 3

# *Assembly and Layout*

At this point, you've gathered all the necessary information for your resume, and you've rewritten it using the language necessary to impress potential employers. Your next step is to assemble these elements in a logical order and lay them out on the page neatly and attractively to achieve the desired effect: getting that interview.

## Assembly

The order of the elements in a resume makes a difference in its overall effect. Obviously, you would not want to put your name and address in the middle of the resume or your special skills section at the top. You want to put the elements in an order that stresses your most important achievements, not the less pertinent information. For example, if you recently graduated from school and have no full-time work experience, you will want to list your education before you list any part-time jobs you may have held during school. On the other hand, if you have been gainfully employed for several years and currently hold an important position in your company, you will want to list your work experience ahead of your education, which has become less pertinent with time.

Some elements are always included in your resume, and some are optional. Following is a list of essential and optional elements:

|                **Essential**                |                **Optional**                |
|---------------------------|---------------------------|
| Name                      | Job Objective             |
| Address                   | Honors                    |
| Phone Number              | Special Skills            |
| Work Experience           | Professional Memberships  |
| Education                 | Activities                |
|                           | Certificates and Licenses |
|                           | Personal Information      |
|                           | References Phrase         |

Your choice of optional sections depends on your own background and employment needs. Always use information that puts you and your abilities in a favorable light. If your honors are impressive, include them in your resume. If your activities in school demonstrate particular talents necessary for the job you are seeking, then allow space for a section on activities. Each resume is unique, just as each person is unique.

## Types of Resumes

So far, our discussion about resumes has involved the most common type—the *reverse chronological* resume (see example on page 22), in which your most recent job is listed first and so on. This is the type of resume usually preferred by human resources directors, and it is the one most frequently used. However, in some cases this style of presentation is not the most effective way to highlight your skills and accomplishments.

For someone reentering the workforce after many years or someone looking to change career fields, the *functional resume* may work best (see example on page 23). This type of resume focuses more on achievement and less on the sequence of your work history. In the functional resume, your experience is presented by what you have accomplished and the skills you have developed in your past work.

Assemble a functional resume from the same information you collected for your chronological resume. The main difference lies in how you organize this information. Essentially, the work experience section becomes two sections, with your job duties and accomplishments comprising one section and your employer's name, city, state, your position, and the dates employed making up another section. Place the first section near the top of the resume, just below the job objective section, and call it *Accomplishments* or *Achievements*. The second section, containing the bare essentials of your employment history, should come after the accomplishments section and can be titled *Work Experience* or *Employment History*. The other sections of your resume remain the same. The work experience section is the only one affected in the functional resume. By placing the section that focuses on your achievements first, you draw attention to these achievements. This puts less emphasis on who you worked for and more emphasis on what you did and what you are capable of doing.

For someone changing careers, emphasis on skills and achievements is essential. The identities of previous employers, which may be unrelated to one's new job field, need to be downplayed. The functional resume accomplishes this task. For someone reentering the workforce after many years, a functional resume is the obvious choice. If you lack full-time work experience, you will need to draw attention away from this fact and instead focus on your skills and abilities gained possibly through volunteer activities or part-time work. Education may also play a more important role in this resume.

The type of resume that is right for you depends on your own personal circumstances. It may be helpful to create a chronological *and* a functional resume and then compare the two to find out which is more suitable. The sample resumes found in this book include both chronological and functional resumes. Use these resumes as guides to help you decide on the content and appearance of your own resume.

## Layout

Once you have decided which elements to include in your resume and have arranged them in an order that makes sense and emphasizes your achievements and abilities, it is time to work on the physical layout of your resume.

There is no single appropriate layout that applies to every resume, but there are a few basic rules to follow in putting your resume on paper:

1. Leave a comfortable margin on the sides, top, and bottom of the page (usually 1 to 1½ inches).

2. Use appropriate spacing between the sections (usually 2 to 3 line spaces are adequate).

3. Be consistent in the *type* of headings you use for the different sections of your resume. For example, if you capitalize the heading EMPLOYMENT HISTORY, don't use initial capitals and underlining for a heading of equal importance, such as <u>Education</u>.

# CHRONOLOGICAL RESUME

**Matthew L. Scott**
**590 La Honda**
**Palo Alto, CA 94307**
**415-555-7359**

## BUSINESS EXPERIENCE

**1993–present**          **Hewlett Packard, Inc.**

*Corporate Treasurer (9/94–present)*
Responsible for cash management, foreign exchange, investing, bank relations, financing activities, insurance and risk management, and taxes.
Also responsible for export licensing, international order processing, and international and domestic distribution.

*Assistant Treasurer (1/93–8/94)*
Responsible for taxes, leasing, and special financing projects.

**1990–1992**          **General Instruments**

*Director, Corporate Taxes*
Responsible for all tax matters.

**1987–1989**          **Amdahl Corporation**

*Manager, Domestic Taxes*
Responsible for all corporate tax matters, which included tax planning and research.

**1983–1986**          **Equitable Life Assurance Society**

*Assistant Tax Manager (9/85–11/86)*
Created department to handle all tax research, planning, and audits.

*Assistant East Coast Tax Manager (3/83–8/85)*
Supervised tax compliance.
Performed tax research and planning.
Handled tax audits.

**1980–1982**          **Lowell Properties**

*Assistant Tax Manager*
Responsible for tax compliance, audits, and planning.

**1977–1979**          **Price Waterhouse**

*Senior Tax Accountant*
Performed tax planning, research, and compliance work.

## EDUCATION

M.B.A., University of Chicago, 1977

B.A., Economics, Boston College, 1975

**FUNCTIONAL RESUME**

## Chester Tinsdale
*390 Montana Avenue*
*Albuquerque, NM 87112*
*(505) 555-4168 home*
*(505) 555-1890 office*

### SUMMARY

Extensive experience in commercial and installment loans, branch management, business development, operations, and human resources. Heavy emphasis in credit analysis and portfolio management. Outstanding communicator with ability to establish lasting customer relationships.

### ACCOMPLISHMENTS

- Managed branch office with staff of 20 and $25 million in assets.
- Achieved consistent sales for loans and deposits.
- Increased loan portfolio from $1 million to $10 million in two years.

### EXPERIENCE

1992–present: *Bank of New Mexico*, Albuquerque, NM
Vice President, Commercial Lending Officer
Evaluate financial prospects and manage portfolios covering two counties. Negotiate middle market credits.

1990–1992: *Bank of Phoenix*, Phoenix, AZ
Assistant Branch Manager, Phoenix Corporate Office

1986–1989: *Santa Fe National Bank,* Santa Fe, NM
Vice President and Branch Manager

1970–1985: *First Bank of Albuquerque,* Albuquerque, NM
Successive management and business development positions with this growing bank.

### EDUCATION

B.S., Economics, University of New Mexico
International Banking School, Honors
American Institute of Banking

4. Always try to fit your resume onto one page. If you are having trouble fitting all your information onto one page, perhaps you are trying to say too much. Edit out any repetitive or unnecessary information, shorten descriptions of earlier jobs, and consider that you may have included too many optional sections. Be ruthless.

Don't let the compulsion to tell every detail about your life prevent you from producing a resume that is simple and straightforward. The more compact your resume, the easier it will be to read and the better the impression it will make for you.

In some cases, the resume will not fit on a single page, even after extensive editing. In such cases, the resume should be printed on two pages so as not to compromise clarity or appearance. Each page of a two-page resume should be marked clearly with your name and the page number, for example, "Judith Ramirez, page 1 of 2." The pages should be stapled together.

Experiment with various layouts until you find one that looks good to you. Always show your final layout to other people and ask them what they like or dislike about it and what impresses them most about your resume. Make sure that is what you want most to emphasize. If it isn't, you may want to consider making changes in your layout until the necessary information is emphasized. Use the sample resumes in this book to get some ideas for laying out your resume.

## Putting Your Resume in Print

Your resume should be printed on good quality $8\frac{1}{2}'' \times 11''$ bond paper. You want to make as good an impression as possible with your resume; therefore, quality paper is a necessity. If you have access to a word processor with a good printer or know of someone who does, make use of it. Typewritten resumes should be used only when there are no other options available.

After you have produced a clean original, make duplicate copies of it. Usually a copy shop is your best bet for producing copies without smudges or streaks. Have the copy shop use quality bond paper for all copies of your resume, and ask for a sample copy before they run your entire order. After copies are made, check each copy for cleanliness and clarity.

Another, more costly, option is to have your resume typeset and printed by a printer. This provides the most attractive resume of all. If you anticipate needing a lot of copies of your resume, the cost of having it typeset may be justified.

## Proofreading

After you have finished typing the master copy of your resume and before you have it copied or printed, thoroughly check it for typing and spelling errors. Have several people read it over just in case you have missed an error. Misspelled words and typing mistakes do not make a good impression on a prospective employer, as they reflect badly on your writing ability and your attention to detail. With thorough and conscientious proofreading, these mistakes can be avoided.

The following are some rules of capitalization and punctuation that may come in handy when proofreading your resume:

### RULES OF CAPITALIZATION

- Capitalize proper nouns, such as names of schools, colleges, and universities; names of companies; and brand names of products.

- Capitalize major words in the names and titles of books, tests, and articles that appear in the body of your resume.

- Capitalize words in major section headings of your resume.

- Do not capitalize words just because they seem important.

- When in doubt, consult a manual of style such as *Words into Type* (Prentice Hall) or *The Chicago Manual of Style* (The University of Chicago Press). Your local library can help you locate these and other reference books.

### RULES OF PUNCTUATION

- Use a comma to separate words in a series.

- Use a semicolon to separate series of words that already include commas within the series.

- Use a semicolon to separate independent clauses that are not joined by a conjunction.

- Use a period to end a sentence.

- Use a colon to show that examples or details follow that will expand or amplify the preceding phrase.

- Avoid the use of dashes.

- Avoid the use of brackets.

- If you use any punctuation in an unusual way in your resume, be consistent in its use.

- Whenever you are uncertain, consult a style manual.

# *The Cover Letter*

Once your resume has been assembled, laid out, and printed to your satisfaction, the final step before distribution is to write your cover letter. Though there may be instances when you deliver your resume in person, you usually send it through the mail. Resumes sent through the mail always need an accompanying letter that briefly introduces you and your resume. The purpose of the cover letter is to get a potential employer to read your resume, just as the purpose of your resume is to get that same potential employer to call you for an interview.

Like your resume, your cover letter should be clean, neat, and direct. A cover letter usually includes the following information:

1. Your name and address (unless it already appears on your personal letterhead).

2. The date.

3. The name and address of the person and company to whom you are sending your resume.

4. The salutation ("Dear Mr." or "Dear Ms." followed by the person's last name, or "To Whom It May Concern" if you are answering a blind ad).

5. An opening paragraph explaining why you are writing (for example: in response to an ad, the result of a previous meeting, at the suggestion of someone you both know) and indicating that you are interested in the job being offered.

6. One or two more paragraphs that tell why you want to work for the company and what qualifications and experience you can bring to that company.

7. A final paragraph that closes the letter and requests that you be contacted for an interview. You may mention here that your references are available upon request.

8. The closing ("Sincerely," or "Yours truly," followed by your signature with your name typed under it).

Your cover letter, including all of the information above, should be no more than one page in length. The language used should be polite, businesslike, and to the point. Do not attempt to tell your life story in the cover letter. A long and cluttered letter will only serve to put off the reader. Remember, you need to mention only a few of your accomplishments and skills in the cover letter. The rest of your information is in the resume. If your cover letter is a success, your resume will be read and all pertinent information reviewed by your prospective employer.

## Producing the Cover Letter

Cover letters should always be individualized, since they are always written to particular individuals and companies. Never use a form letter for your cover letter. Each one should be as personal as possible. Of course, once you have written and rewritten your first cover letter until you are satisfied with it, you can certainly use similar wording in subsequent letters.

After you have typed your cover letter on quality bond paper, proofread it as thoroughly as you did your resume. Again, spelling errors are a sure sign of carelessness, and you don't want that to be a part of the first impression you give a prospective employer. Handle the letter and resume carefully to avoid any smudges, and then mail both your cover letter and resume in an appropriately sized envelope. Keep an accurate record of all the resumes you send out and the results of each mailing.

Numerous sample cover letters appear at the end of this book. Use them as models for your own cover letter or to get an idea of how cover letters are put together. Remember, every cover letter is unique and depends on the particular circumstances of the individual writing it and the job for which he or she is applying.

About a week after mailing resumes and cover letters to potential employers, contact them by telephone. Confirm that your resume arrived, and ask whether an interview is possible. This makes you appear organized and genuinely interested in the position for which you are applying. Getting your foot in the door during this call is an important part of landing a job, and a strong resume and cover letter will help you immeasurably.

# Chapter 5

# *Sample Resumes*

This chapter contains dozens of sample resumes for people pursuing a wide variety of jobs and careers within the banking and financial industries.

There are many different styles of resumes in terms of graphic layout and presentation of information. These samples also represent people with varying amounts of education and work experience. Model your own resume after these samples. Choose one resume or borrow elements from several different resumes to help you construct your own.

## MARTA GOMEZ

*46 Lafayette Street, #18*
*New Orleans, LA 70118*
*(504) 555-1260 home*
*(504) 555-8989 cell*

**Objective:**     A position in public accounting that uses my knowledge of tax accounting and international business.

**Education:**     A. B. Freeman School of Business, Tulane University, New Orleans, LA.
Master of Accounting degree with emphasis in tax law, December 2000. GPA: 4.0

University of Texas, Austin, TX.
Bachelor of Science, Business Administration, with emphasis in accounting and finance, May 2000. GPA: 4.0

**Honors:**        Dean's List
Academic Achievement Award

**Memberships:**   Beta Alpha Psi, National Honorary Accounting Fraternity
Beta Gamma Sigma, National Scholastic Honor Society for Collegiate Schools of Business.

**Activities:**    Volunteer, Income Tax Assistance Program.
Participant in annual singing and music festivals.
Piano playing and singing.

**Experience:**    Project Assistant, Tulane University. Prepare monthly reports of university funds. Tutor students in Managerial Cost Accounting. (June 2000 to present.)

Student Accountant, University of Texas Press, Austin, TX. Prepared monthly managerial reports and financial statements. Maintained cash disbursements journal and performed bookkeeping. (September 1999 to April 2000.)

Accounting Clerk, International Transportation, Mexico City, Mexico. Performed data entry and bookkeeping. (June 1999 to July 1999.)

**Additional
Information:**     Fluent in Spanish and Portuguese.
Studied in Brazil for one year.
Comfortable with world travel and multicultural communication.

# PAIGE GRAHAM

*86 Wilshire Blvd., # 8C*
*Los Angeles, CA 90024*
*Home: (310) 555-1326*
*Cell: (310) 555-9834*

## PROFESSIONAL EXPERIENCE

*Grubb and Ellis, Santa Monica, CA*
*Administrative Assistant to Managing Broker, from 10/99 to present*
Supervise daily activities of office; process listings, sales, and closings of properties; coordinate advertising; compute rents and commissions; review and answer mail; operate office equipment.

*Paul of Pasadena, Pasadena, CA*
*Office Manager, from 2/98 to 9/99*
Managed office operations for busy salon; scheduled meetings and travel arrangements; conducted high volume personal and telephone contact with clients; trained 10 sales consultants; controlled salon's inventory, displays, and promotions.

*Japan Trade Institute, Washington, DC*
*Researcher, from 9/97 to 12/97*
Researched, wrote, and produced monthly publications; provided information on U.S.–Japan economic, political, and legal trade issues.

*Capitol Hill Center, Washington, DC*
*Administrative Assistant to Program Administrator, from 10/95 to 7/97*
Developed database of national faculty advisors, updated current listings of national colleges, and scheduled students for "Washington, DC Series" forums.

## PUBLICATIONS AND HONORS

Contributed review of *Gai-Jin* in *The Asian Reporter*, 2000
Delegate to Model United Nations, national conference, New York, NY, 1998
Recipient, Douglas MacArthur Scholarship to Japan, 1997
Participant in Rotary Youth Exchange to Japan, 1996
Representative of Japan in the United States Student Organization, 1995

## EDUCATION

University of California, Berkeley, 1995
Bachelor of Arts, International Relations; Minor in Asian Studies
Coursework: Japanese Language, International Business, Pacific Basin Studies

**References Available Upon Request.**

## JACK STETSON

680 Grinnell Drive
Des Moines, Iowa 50316
(515) 555-3600 home
(515) 555-9980 cellular

### *OBJECTIVE*

Administrative management position in the operations and information processing functions of a financial services company.

### *HIGHLIGHTS OF QUALIFICATIONS*

- Almost 15 years of bank management experience in retail and operational areas.
- Eight years of executive bank management experience.
- Demonstrated record of performance and reliability.
- Highly skilled in people management and situational analysis.

### *SKILLS AND EXPERIENCE*

PROJECTS/PROGRAMS

- Managed the feasibility analysis, installation, and start-up of an automated teller system.
- Developed standard procedures, accountability mechanisms, and operating criteria for an in-house data processing system.
- Managed the operational factors in the sale and purchase of mortgage loan portfolios.
- Coordinated the physical move of a bank headquarters facility.
- Developed and managed a program of product changes and new service fees which tripled service charge income in two years.

ADMINISTRATION/MANAGEMENT

- Directed all the functional aspects of bank deposit and transaction accounting.
- Supervised daily activities of 70 staff members and 10 midlevel managers.
- Experienced in cash management function.
- Developed a salary administration policy and a job pricing mechanism.
- Participated in the development of professional conduct, smoking, and dress policies.

*Jack Stetson—page one of two*

## EMPLOYMENT HISTORY

| | |
|---|---|
| 1996–present | Vice President, Senior Operations Officer |
| | Railroadmen's Banking Company |
| | Des Moines, Iowa |
| 1993–1996 | Vice President, Senior Operations Officer |
| | United Federal Savings & Loan |
| | Dubuque, Iowa |
| 1991–1993 | Vice President, Bank Operations |
| | First National Bank |
| | Terre Haute, Indiana |
| 1987–1991 | Branch Officer and Manager |
| | Iowa National Bank |
| | Sioux City, Iowa |
| 1985–1987 | Production Supervisor |
| | General Electric |
| | Davenport, Iowa |

## EDUCATION AND TRAINING

University of Iowa, B.S., Business Administration, 1985

Certificate from Electronics Telecommunications School of Midwestern Telephone

Six classes completed at Management and Technology School, General Electric

Several technical and administrative seminars at Iowa Bankers Association

*Jack Stetson—page two of two*

# Dennis Sutton

1691 South Lake Shore Drive
Chicago, IL 60610
(312) 555-1511
E-mail: dsutton@xxx.net

## Education

M.B.A., Finance, June 2001, University of Chicago, Chicago, IL
B.S., Civil Engineering, 1995, Rose-Hulman Institute of Technology,
Terre Haute, IN

## Experience

Summer 2000, Continental Securities, Chicago, IL
ASSOCIATE IN CORPORATE FINANCE DEPARTMENT: Performed detailed valuation analysis, drafting of sales memorandum, and due diligence analysis for a major divestiture. Prepared client presentation for initial public offering, which included a discussion of equity market conditions and comparable trading and valuation multiples.

1997–1999, G & T Engineers, Chicago, IL
PROJECT ENGINEER: Prepared contract drawings, bid booklets, preliminary design investigation, and final design for street and bridge improvements. Supervised two engineers and one draftsman. Projects included Eisenhower Expressway, Ohio Street, and Michigan Avenue parking facility.

1995–1997, Department of Transportation, Chicago, IL
PROJECT MANAGER: Developed and implemented management plan for rehabilitation of infrastructure. Performed field investigation and determined project scope, schedules, and budgets.

## References Available Upon Request.

# Sarah Thatcher

3245 Forest Drive
Salem, OR 97301
(503) 555-4982 home

**Summary:**

Over 10 years of experience in consumer and commercial lending, business development, and operations. Proven ability to provide full range of customer services.

**Major Accomplishments:**

- Helped merchants to consistently exceed their goals.
- Developed formal cross-selling program.
- Wrote training manual for merchant card services.

## EXPERIENCE

1998–present  FIRST STATE BANK, Salem, OR
**Assistant Vice President**—Loan Offices

- Analyze and structure commercial, real estate, construction, and installment loans.
- Returned merchant card portfolio to profitability.

1997–1998  OREGON BANKCARD, Portland, OR
**Assistant Manager**—Merchant Card Services

- Managed merchant card portfolio.
- Developed operational procedures.
- Directed work flow to subordinate staff.

1994–1997  ALLIED BANK OF OREGON, Eugene, OR
**Personal Banking Manager**

- Maintained and developed commercial and installment loan portfolio.

1992–1994  ALLIED BANK OF OREGON, Bend, OR
**Personal Banking Manager**

- Responsible for loan portfolio documentation.
- Supervised note department.

1991—1992  ALLIED BANK OF OREGON, Portland, OR
**Senior Note Clerk**

- Responsible for documentation, posting, and balancing.

## EDUCATION

University of Oregon, Eugene, OR, two years
Chemeketa Community College, Salem, OR, one year

**MARKITA C. NEWMAN**

**60 Cape Cod Court**

**Providence, RI 02912**

**(401) 555-7050**

Over 20 years' experience in loan management, financial planning and management, and administrative functions.

**EXPERIENCE**

| | |
|---|---|
| March 1994 - present | *Providence Security Bank, Providence, RI* <br> Successively: <br> • Construction Loan Officer <br> • Commercial Loan Officer <br> • Senior Loan Officer <br> • Assistant Vice President |
| October 1990 - February 1994 | *R & R Investment Company, Providence, RI* <br> Senior Investment Executive |
| February 1981 - October 1990 | *Continental Bank, Hartford, CT* <br> Successively: <br> • Bank Management Training Program Trainee <br> • Credit Officer <br> • Senior Loan Officer <br> • Assistant Vice President–Branch Manager |

**EDUCATION**

| | |
|---|---|
| 2000 | *East Coast Banking School, Boston, MA* <br> Certificate of Completion |
| 1984 - 1986 | *University of Hartford, West Hartford, CT* <br> MBA Program |
| 1981 | *Roger Williams College, Bristol, RI* <br> B.S., Business Administration |

# LLOYD W. THOMPSON

| Present Address (until January 2001) | Permanent Address |
|---|---|
| *68 Spring Street* | *560 El Cerro* |
| *Los Angeles, CA 90024* | *Danville, CA 94526* |
| *(510) 555-6300* | *(510) 555-4630* |

## EXPERIENCE:

Summer 2000
Goldman Sachs, New York, NY
Fixed Income Department
**Associate**
Tracked financial performance of telecommunications and media industries. Identified relative value trends in corporate bond market. Presented findings to institutional sales force, traders, and corporate finance staff.

1995–1998
Bankers Trust, New York, NY
Merchant Banking
**Account Executive**
Responsible for investing in LBO senior and subordinated debt and equity. Monitored portfolio investments in manufacturing, retail, consumer products, and energy industries. Assisted in restructuring and bankruptcy.

## EDUCATION:

Anderson Graduate School of Management at UCLA, M.B.A., 2000
Member, Investment Finance Club, Toastmasters, and Riordan Program

Stanford University, B.A., French, 1995

## ADDITIONAL INFORMATION:

Fluent in French.
Extensive knowledge of Microsoft Excel, Word, and WordPerfect.

## REFERENCES:

Available upon request.

# EMMA R. THORNTON

23965 East 26th Street
Salt Lake City, UT 84113
(801) 555-4197 home
(801) 555-9823 cell phone

## Work History

1997–present        Utah Consulting Group, Salt Lake City, UT, **Consultant.**

Improved computer-based model to derive cash flow and debt service for collateralized mortgage obligations.

Performed return analysis for potential investor of commercial office building.

Redesigned database software for residential and commercial mortgage loans' engagements.

1995–1996        K.L. Gifford & Associates, Boston, MA, **Associate.**

Worked on finance, acquisitions, and marketing assignments.

Implemented a dividend reinvestment program.

Developed new promotional material for expanded marketing effort.

## Education

1990–1995        University of Idaho, Moscow, ID
Bachelor of Science in Economics and Finance
Grade point average: 3.8/4.0

*Available for work immediately.*

**Darien Granger**
**10596 Wildwood Drive**
**Milwaukee, WI 53202**
**(414) 555-2639 home phone**
**(414) 555-9089 cell phone**

### Summary of Qualifications

Driven, results-oriented, and effective professional with over 20 years of experience in banking operations.

### Professional History

**Milwaukee National Bank,** Milwaukee, WI

1997 to present

*Senior Operations Officer*

- Supervise all operations of the office.
- Implemented a zero deficit policy which resulted in a 50 percent reduction in overtime and eliminated operational losses.
- Hire and train operations staff.
- Conduct performance reviews of all personnel.

**Madison State Bank,** Madison, WI

1987 to 1997

*Operations Officer*

- Directed operations of the office, staff of 10.

**First National Bank of Madison,** Madison, WI

1979 to 1987

*Operations Officer*

- Trained staff on new computer system.
- Supervised data processing center functions which included check filing, general ledger, courier service, and return item processing.

### Educational Background

1974 to 1978, University of Wisconsin, Madison, WI

B.S., Computer Science

## Chester Tinsdale

*390 Montana Avenue*
*Albuquerque, NM 87112*
*(505) 555-4168 home*
*(505) 555-1890 office*

## SUMMARY

Extensive experience in commercial and installment loans, branch management, business development, operations, and human resources. Heavy emphasis in credit analysis and portfolio management. Outstanding communicator with ability to establish lasting customer relationships.

## ACCOMPLISHMENTS

- Managed branch office with staff of 20 and $25 million in assets.
- Achieved consistent sales for loans and deposits.
- Increased loan portfolio from $1 million to $10 million in two years.

## EXPERIENCE

1992–present: *Bank of New Mexico*, Albuquerque, NM
Vice President, Commercial Lending Officer
Evaluate financial prospects and manage portfolios covering two counties. Negotiate middle market credits.

1990–1992: *Bank of Phoenix*, Phoenix, AZ
Assistant Branch Manager, Phoenix Corporate Office

1986–1989: *Santa Fe National Bank*, Santa Fe, NM
Vice President and Branch Manager

1970–1985: *First Bank of Albuquerque*, Albuquerque, NM
Successive management and business development positions with this growing bank.

## EDUCATION

B.S., Economics, University of New Mexico
International Banking School, Honors
American Institute of Banking

# MARGARET STOKELY

**3215 CREEKSIDE LANE**
**ATLANTA, GA 30314**
**(404) 555-4928**

## OBJECTIVE

A challenging position in the financial sector.

## EMPLOYMENT EXPERIENCE

7/00–present, Bank of Georgia

*Customer Service Representative*

Responsibilities include customer service,
cash drawer balancing, and other administrative duties.

5/98–6/00, First Bank of the South

*Administrative Assistant*

Responsibilities included organizing shareholders' meetings,
attending banking trade shows, typing, filing, and answering phones.

12/96–5/98, Equitable Life Assurance

*Remittance Clerk*

Responsibilities included processing incoming checks
and daily recording of amounts collected.

6/95–11/96, Equitable Life Assurance

*Customer Service Representative*

Responsibilities included processing claims,
handling current insurance customers' needs, and updating files.

1/93–5/95, Equitable Life Assurance

*Assistant to the Supervisor*

Responsibilities included answering phones,
typing correspondence, and assisting the supervisor as necessary.

## EDUCATION

Georgia Southwestern College, Americus, GA:
B.A. in English, 1993

## REFERENCES

Available upon request.

# GLORIA WINTERS

3424 Cypress Drive • Portland, OR 97203 • (503) 555-6541

## EXPERIENCE

**Academy of Design College,** Portland, OR

1996–present  Chief Financial Officer

Responsible for the financial, accounting, computer, and personnel functions.

- Negotiate bank lines of credit, equipment leases, service contracts, and governmental student financial aid.

- Improved overall operating efficiency.

- Developed a formalized budgeting and planning process.

**Pacific Insurance Corporation,** Portland, OR

1993–1996  Director of Accounting

Responsible for financial reporting and review of the company's accounting function.

- Consolidated monthly financial information from the different divisions.

- Provided financial recommendations to senior management.

- Analyzed business trends and variances.

1990–1993  Accounting Manager—Financial Planning

- Developed financial model that coordinated accounting, treasury, and tax staffs.

**Deloitte & Touche,** Portland, OR

1983–1990  Supervisor Accountant

Responsible for the planning, organization, and completion of audits.

*Gloria Winters—page one of two*

## EDUCATION

Reed College, Portland, OR
Bachelor of Arts in Economics, 1983

## REFERENCES

Available upon request.

**HANS AAMODTSON**                          *800 Green Street, Apartment 8*
                                            *New York, NY 10014*
                                            *(212) 555-9611 (home)*
                                            *(212) 555-5570 (work)*

**PROFESSIONAL EXPERIENCE:**

**Merrill Lynch & Co., Inc.,** New York, NY
**Director,** 1995 - Present
Manager of investment strategy and alternative investment products, Private Advisory Services
- Developed proprietary fund of funds products
- Responsible for sales effort of institutional private partnership transactions to middle market
- Developed proprietary HNW investment strategy platform; head of HNW investment committee
- Established systems and procedures to manage, track, and coordinate cross-selling initiatives
- Coordinate ongoing training of proprietary sales teams and financial consultants through presentations and joint calling efforts
- Developed and implemented primary calling effort to new clients

**Bankers Trust Company,** New York, NY
**Vice President,** 1993 - 1995
Manager of a global joint venture between the Private Bank and the Investment Bank
- Started new effort to cross-sell corporate finance services to privately held companies
- Trained Private Bank's relationship managers through presentations and joint calling efforts
- Established systems and procedures to coordinate global cross-selling initiatives
- Brought institutional products to the individual HNW market place
- Originated corporate finance transactions for private and closely held companies
- Coordinated with worldwide product and industry experts to secure and execute client mandates

**Swiss Bank Corporation Investment Banking, Inc.,** New York, NY
**Financial Analyst,** 1992 - 1993
Cross-border M&A and equity placements, utilizing the same analytical and technical skills as at Kidder, Peabody

**Kidder, Peabody & Co. Incorporated,** New York, NY
**Financial Analyst,** 1990 - 1992
Worked as generalist in corporate finance (1990 - 1991) and in the Asia Pacific Group (1991 - 1992)
- Developed projections and business plans for existing companies and start-up ventures
- Created financial models to show the pro forma effects of financings, mergers, and acquisitions
- Conducted market and industry research, prepared published research reports on multi-national development banks
- Prepared comparable company and transaction valuations and discounted cash flow analyses
- Prepared public and private offering documents

**Norwegian Armed Forces,** Sessvold, Norway
**Officer School (Special Forces),** 1986 - 1987
- Ranked "Best Recruit" and selected as an instructor to the elite royal ski platoon

## EDUCATION:

**University of Michigan,** Ann Arbor, MI
B.A. with Distinction and High Honors in Economics, Dean's list
- Wrote honors thesis on the effect of OPEC policy on oil prices

**University of Trondheim,** Trondheim, Norway
Examen Philosoficum

**Trondheim College of Economics & Business Administration,** Trondheim, Norway
Coursework toward a Business Administration degree
- Ranked first in a class of 150 students
- Elected to the board of the student government

**United World College of Southeast Asia,** Republic of Singapore
International Baccalaureate
- Selected as National Scholar by the Norwegian National Committee
- Wrote extended essay on the empirical effects of monetary policies in Norway

## TRANSACTIONS:

**Bankers Trust Company**
Selected and originated mandates:
- Valuation and exclusive sale assignments for a privately held uniform manufacturer ($50 million)
- Sell-side advisory for a West Coast beverage distributor ($25 million)
- Financing and equity investment for a distressed loan purchaser ($25 million)
- Buy-side mandate and IPO for a privately owned railroad ($75 million)
- High yield bond offering for a privately owned P&C insurance company ($80 million)
- Sell-side mandate for a real estate management company ($100 million)
- Private placement for a European private university ($50 million)
- Refinancing assignment for a privately held aircraft maintenance company ($80 million)
- High yield bond offering and secondary offering for Latin American regional telephone company ($100 million)

**Swiss Bank Corporation Investment Banking Inc.**
Completed transactions:
- Bank of East Asia 144a equity placement
- PT Mayora Indah 144a equity placement
- $1.8 billion secondary equity offering for Chrysler Corporation
- $110 million IPO for Financial Security Assurance Holdings Ltd.
- Advisory for minority investment in public UK company

**Kidder, Peabody & Co. Incorporated**
Completed transactions:
- $105 million American Depository Receipts offering for Orbital Engine Corporation
- $20 million Dual Currency Convertible Loan placement for GITIC
- Three Notes offerings for the African Development Bank, totaling $800 million
- $300 million Notes offering for the Inter-American Development Bank
- $1 billion MTN Program for the Electricity Corporation of New Zealand
- Financial advisory and $150 million MTN Program for Washington Gas & Light Co.

# Joanne L. Vaughn

| **CURRENT ADDRESS** | **PERMANENT ADDRESS** |
|---|---|
| P.O. Box 642 | 12091 Santa Fe Boulevard |
| Dallas, TX 75275 | Austin, TX 78704 |
| (214) 555-1281 | (512) 555-4363 |

## OBJECTIVE

To use my language and people skills in a challenging position within the banking and financial services field.

## EDUCATION

Southern Methodist University (SMU), Dallas, TX
B.A. in Political Science and Spanish expected May 2001
GPA in majors: 3.2 and 3.9 respectively

## EXPERIENCE

*Programming Director, Cable 20 SMU Community Television.* 2000–present
- Assemble and determine the programming for student-run cable station.
- Recommend programming proposal to production staff.
- Maintain station's image through the choice of programming.

*Assistant, Spanish Language Lab, SMU.* 2000–2001 school year
- Assisted students in using software language lessons.
- Supervised the daily lab operations.

*Office Assistant, Intramural Sports Program, SMU.* 1999–2000 school year.
- Acted as liaison between program director and students.
- Prepared expense reports, travel itineraries, and sport event schedules.

*Bookstore Clerk, SMU Bookstore.* Summer 2001
- Priced and stocked books, conducted summer inventory.
- Placed fall book orders, and maintained computerized bookstore listing.

## ACTIVITIES

- Exchange Student, Guadalajara, Mexico, Summer 2000
- Exchange Student, Madrid, Spain, Summer 1999
- Big Sister Program
- Freshman Advisor
- SMU Tour Guide
- Rafting and swimming

# DUNCAN McCLOUD

3980 ADMIRAL WAY
BALTIMORE, MD 21210
(301) 555-8568

*Objective:*

A position in the tax department of a national public accounting firm.

*Experience:*

**Heart Rehabilitation Program,** 1999–2000
Baltimore, MD
Associate Accountant
- Responsible for accounting and system development.
- Designed payroll processing system that improved accuracy and reduced computation time.

**Maryland Bell,** 1998–1999
Baltimore, MD
Finance Intern
- Computed and billed office services and computer lab costs to appropriate project cost centers.
- Audited departmental purchase requisitions.

**Commercial Properties, Inc.,** Summer 1998
Rockville, MD
Sales Intern
- Gathered information on Baltimore area retail properties to project market rents.

**Olive Garden,** 1996–1998
Washington, DC
Area Supervisor
- Managed restaurant activities in the DC area.
- Hired and trained restaurant employees.

**Peace Corps,** 1995–1996
Philippines
Volunteer

*Education:*

Oberlin College, Oberlin, OH
B.A., Anthropology, 1995.

*Interests:*

Skiing, mountain climbing, and golf

*References:*

Furnished on request

Antonia Rutherford                          E-mail: erutherford@xxx.net
7900 Mile High Ave.                              807-555-4949 home
Salt Lake City, UT 84126                         807-555-2911 cell

### GOAL:

Vice President of Operations at a reputable banking institution.

### ACHIEVEMENTS:

- Assisted Senior Vice President in day-to-day operations
- Directed work procedures in light of bank policy
- Managed assets, securities, and bank records
- Established all operating procedures and policies in the department
- Coordinated duties of department personnel
- Served on bank policy review board
- Assisted in the planning of branch locations
- Handled accounting and financial analysis
- Approved and declined credit for loans

### WORK HISTORY:

First National Bank of Utah, Salt Lake City, UT
Assistant Vice President, 1988–present

First National Bank of Utah, Provo, UT
Branch Director, 1983–1988

Santa Fe Bank, Santa Fe, NM
Teller, 1982–1983

### EDUCATION:

Washington State University, Pullman, WA
B.S. in Accounting, 1980

*References available on request*

ANN MORI
32 Kapalua Way
Honolulu, HI 96822
(808) 555-4316
E-mail address: annmori@xxx.com

---

## SUMMARY

An experienced professional with strong analytical and administrative skills. Proven performer across organizational lines.

---

## PROFESSIONAL EXPERIENCE

Pacific Bank - Honolulu, HI, 1996–present.

*Commercial Loan Officer,* 2000–present.
- Responsible for developing new commercial business loans and servicing existing customers.
- Wrote credit reports and recommended appropriate action.
- Supervised lobby staff, loan clerks, and account representatives.

*Assistant Personnel Manager,* 1996–2000.
- Responsible for staffing and policy guidelines.
- Coordinated policy changes.
- Directed payroll and benefits functions.
- Assisted in the integration of employee benefits, payroll, and related functions.

---

## EDUCATION AND TRAINING

Courses at Hilo Community College and Hawaii Pacific College
- Analysis of Financial Statements
- Business Communication
- Business Accounting
- Real Estate Principles
- Computer Science

Professional Courses
- Credit Analysis I and II
- Commercial Loan Documentation
- Website Design and Management

*CARLOS RODRIGUEZ*
*68 Via Robles Drive*
*Valencia, CA 91355*
*(805) 555-6050 home*
*(805) 555-9900 cellular*

## Summary of Experience

- Extensive experience in credit analysis, investments, and planning.

- Skilled at developing and retaining customer relationships through innovative and professional service.

- Designed new security and foreign exchange trading activities.

- Assisted a major Japanese bank in opening operations in California.

- Produced a 25 percent return on equity with the "account officer" concept.

- Adept at achieving a balance between authority and accountability.

- Able to promote staff initiative and participation as members of a team.

## Experience

### Finance and Banking Consultant, Tokai Bank of California (1994 - present)

Work with board of directors and senior management to review the financial institution's organizational structure, to set up management by objectives, to perform competitive analysis, and to organize credit departments according to the account officer concept. Train account officers in customer calling, loan negotiations, credit presentation writing, and techniques to monitor loan documentation compliance.

Have offered consulting services to seven financial institutions. The most recent assignment involved a newly restructured bank. By implementing the account officer concept and focusing on key exporters, the bank grew to $30 million in assets with a 25 percent return on equity.

### Senior Consultant, Agricultural Cooperatives Union (1992 - 1994)

- Analyzed current and future financial requirements and the cooperatives' ability to offer commercial banking services.

- Developed complete financial projections and assisted in setting up a banking subsidiary that opened in September 1992.

### Management Responsibilities with Wells Fargo (1976 - 1992)

*Manager of a wholly owned financial subsidiary*

- Promoted arbitrage of government-backed securities between issuer and final buyer.

- Issued performance bonds.

- Set up foreign exchange activities.

- Initiated new financial activities.

*C. Rodriguez—page one of two*

*Vice President of finance company*

- Established a $40 million industrial and commercial loan portfolio that achieved consistent returns.

*Credit Supervisor:*

- Reviewed credit requests beyond the credit limits of their accounts; decided on appropriate recommendation.

*General Loan Officer:*

- Implemented format for quick review of bank's single major exposures.

*Syndicate Loan Officer:*

- Designed computerized loan service system.

## Education

Bachelor of Science, Economics, University of Madrid, Spain, 1976.

## References

Furnished on request.

ERIC C. LAWTON

*24961 Erie Parkway*
*Cleveland, Ohio 44106*
*Home (216) 555-4971*

## OBJECTIVE

To provide financial services on an interim basis to moderately sized companies as financial consultant in the capacity of Chief Financial Officer.

## EXPERIENCE/ACCOMPLISHMENTS

**Lawton Advisors,** Cleveland, Ohio                                1999 to present
   *President*
Provide financial consulting services to moderately sized companies.

**ModComputer Inc.,** Cleveland, Ohio                               1996 to 1999
   *Chief Financial Officer*
ModComputer is a venture capital-backed computer equipment manufacturer with annual revenues of $15 million.

Responsible for Finance and Human Resources. In charge of general accounting, cost accounting, financial planning, profit and loss management, credit and collection, and financial reporting. Evaluated potential mergers and acquisitions. Led the firm to its first profitable quarter in five years. Negotiated key leases and business contracts which resulted in substantial cost savings. Supervised a staff of 10.

**JTP Instruments, Inc.,** Akron, Ohio                              1986 to 1996
   *Vice President of Finance*                               1990 to 1996
   *Controller*                                             1986 to 1990

JTP is a privately held automotive instrumentation company with annual revenues of $25 million.

Responsible for Finance, Management Information Systems, and Human Resources. In charge of general accounting, cost accounting, financial planning, profit and loss management, external communications, banking relationships, and tax planning. Managed staff of 20.

*Eric Lawton—page one of two*

Directed an average 15 percent growth at high levels of profitability and return on investment. Designed financial control modeling. Created Management Information Systems department. Implemented tax saving concepts and methods for tracking research projects.

| **Columbus Electronics,** Columbus, Ohio | 1983 to 1986 |
| --- | --- |
| *Cost and Systems Manager* | 1984 to 1986 |
| *Cost Accountant* | 1983 to 1984 |

Columbus is a publicly held electronic parts manufacturer with annual revenues of $20 million.

Responsible for general accounting, cost accounting, and data processing functions. Supervised staff of seven.

Directed monthly closing from journal entries to preparation of internal financial statements. Implemented systems for material requirements planning, cost accounting, and general accounting.

| **Erie Steel Corporation,** Cleveland, Ohio | 1981 to 1982 |
| --- | --- |
| *Financial Analyst* | 1982 to 1983 |
| *Cost Accountant* | 1981 to 1982 |

Erie is a privately held manufacturer of fine-grade steel for tools with annual revenues of $30 million.

Responsible for monthly performance analysis, financial statements preparation, forecasting, inventory control, product costing, and cost analysis.

## EDUCATION

M.B.A., Finance, Ohio State University, Columbus, Ohio
B.A., Accounting, Ohio State University, Columbus, Ohio
Certified Public Accountant, Ohio

*DAVID ALLEN POPE*

*7806 Paso Robles Road*
*San Antonio, TX 78284*
*(512) 555-4948*
*E-mail: dap@xxx.net*

**Summary of Experience:**

- Chief Financial Officer of a $90 million privately held company and a start-up e-commerce business.

- Controller of $300 million group, generating $150 million in earnings yearly.

- Thirteen years' experience in software, telecommunications, disk drive, and manufacturing companies.

- Specialist in internal controls, MIS, and cost containment programs.

**Experience:**

***Chief Financial Officer, Focus Computers,*** San Antonio, TX, 2000–2001
Manufacturer of tape, disk, and solid state disk drives. The company has annual revenues of $90 million and employs 500 people worldwide.

- Sold discontinued operation with annual revenues of $10 million.

- Reduced accounts receivable balances by 35 percent.

- Wrote corporate strategic business plan.

- Raised $15 million in new financing offering.

- Eliminated unnecessary operating and manpower costs.

***Chief Financial Officer, Games, Inc.,*** Los Angeles, CA, 2000
Start-up company developing a handheld interactive computer game module and retailing games on company website.

- Implemented computerized financial system and new chart of accounts.

- Responsible for all administrative functions.

- Developed 401(k) benefit plans.

- Provided advice on distribution channels and marketing strategy.

***Controller, Houston Systems,*** Houston, TX, 1998–2000
Seller of UNIX operating systems and other software applications. The family-operated company has annual revenues of $150 million and employs 1,250 people worldwide.

- Installed new general ledger and accounts payable systems and new chart of accounts.

- Defined financial job descriptions, salary levels, and career paths.

- Implemented monthly departmental, sales, and product line profitability reporting.

- Developed intercompany transfer cost strategy.

**Consultant, Compucom,** Austin, TX, 1996–1998
Manufacturer and distributor of modem boards.

- Developed corporate business plan and managed banking and investor relationships.
- Improved computerized financial systems.

**Scott Paper Products,** Los Angeles, CA, 1988–1996
Worked in the packaging group, which included food packaging, plastic film manufacturing, and chemical products.

*Group Controller*
Group included five divisions and 12 manufacturing locations.

- Developed strategic, annual, and capital plans as well as accounting policies and procedures.
- Performed financial valuation for division spin-off.

*Plant Controller*

- Developed plant financial reporting package.
- Increased output by 40 percent and reduced staff by 10 percent.

**Management Consultant, McKinsey and Company**, Los Angeles, CA, 1986–1988
- Developed the consulting practice in Hong Kong.
- Audited and assisted in the preparation of financial and SEC statements.

## Education:

MIT Sloan School of Management, Cambridge, MA: M.B.A., 1986
Princeton University, Princeton, NJ: B.A. in History, 1984

## G. Isaac Schwabacher
310 East 80th Street, #201
New York, NY 10028
(212) 555-4189 (H)
(212) 555-6351 (W)

---

**PROFESSIONAL EXPERIENCE**

### Tax Manager, Deloitte & Touche

December 1997–present
New York, NY

Handle tax planning and research for entertainment, retail sales, and leasing firms. Perform due diligence analysis and financial planning on mergers and acquisitions. Supervise preparation of partnership and corporate tax returns. Review tax provisions for clients. Hire and train professional staff.

### Tax Manager, Coopers & Lybrand

September 1993–December 1997
Albany, NY

**AFFILIATIONS**

Licensed to practice law in New York

Member of the Tax Section, American Bar Association

Member, United Jewish Fund

Volunteer, Business Volunteers for the Arts

**EDUCATION**

J.D., Columbia University Law School, New York, NY, 1993

B.A., Economics, Duke University, Durham, NC, 1990

## Virginia Liu
**48 Pao Boulevard**
**Honolulu, HI 96822**
**(808) 555-8964**

OBJECTIVE

An accounting position in an aggressive results-oriented organization.

EDUCATION

University of Hawaii - B.S. degree in Accounting - 1992

EXPERIENCE

| | |
|---|---|
| 4/98–present | Pong, Evans, & Associates |
| | Honolulu, HI |

*Staff Accountant*
Prepare monthly financial statements, sales tax statements, and income tax returns for clients. Perform audits. Supervise the bookkeeper.

| | |
|---|---|
| 4/92–4/98 | Hawaii Department of Transportation |
| | Honolulu, HI |

*Internal Auditor*
Performed operational, financial, and special audits. Prepared audit reports and audit programs. Updated permanent files, flowcharts, procedures, and policies.

| | |
|---|---|
| 1995–1997 (Part-time) | L & R Glass Company |
| | Honolulu, HI |

*Accountant*
Performed payroll, accounts receivable, and accounts payable accounting operations. Developed proposals for potential clients.

| | |
|---|---|
| 1992–1994 | Hawaii Department of Revenue |
| | Honolulu, HI |

*Tax Examiner*
Performed audit tests on Hawaii tax returns. Implemented training programs for revenue agents who provided taxpayer assistance to the general public.

| | |
|---|---|
| 1992–1994 (Part-time) | Hawaii Pacific College |
| | Honolulu, HI |

*Instructor*
Taught Introduction to Accounting Principles and Business Mathematics.

## JAMES M. MITCHELL

40 Desert Drive • Austin, TX 78705 • (512) 555-4527

### *Objective*

A position as a chief financial officer or corporate treasurer

### *Experience*

**Texas Systems, Austin, TX** (1998–present)

Texas Systems develops, manufactures, and markets automated optical disk-based libraries to OEMs and system integrators.

*Vice President of Finance, Chief Financial Officer*

Raised $20 million in venture capital.
Established business planning and forecasting process.
Developed strategies for initial public offering.
Initiated several programs to increase working capital productivity and arranged the company's first working capital line of credit.
Implemented employee benefit program.

**U.S. West Corporation, Denver, CO** (1997)

*Marketing Manager, PBX Division*

Directed product marketing department
Managed 15 professionals.

**Advanced Systems, Boise, ID** (1986–1997)

*Chief Financial Officer*

Responsible for the controller, treasurer, leasing, tax, internal audit, MIS, and legal functions.

*Vice President of Corporate Development*

Planned entry into new market.

*Vice President of Corporate Marketing*

Responsible for the marketing group as well as sales training, order administration, and promotion.

*Director of Pulp and Paper Marketing*

Directed the marketing and product management for control systems.

*James Mitchell – page one of two*

*Pulping Systems Division Manager*

Implemented marketing programs for the division.

*Area Manager*

Sold process control systems to the pulp and paper industry in the western United States.

**Arthur Andersen & Co., Los Angeles and Tokyo** (1980–1984)

*Consultant*

Consulted in the areas of finance, business planning, and marketing.

## Education

Stanford Graduate School of Business, Stanford, CA (1978)
Master of Business Administration

Worcester Polytechnic Institute, Worcester, MA (1972)
Bachelor of Industrial Engineering with honors

## REFERENCES UPON REQUEST

MARK SCHWARTZ
1469 Pennsylvania Street
Carmel, IN 46032
317-555-2964 (home)
317-555-5717 (work)

**OBJECTIVE:**

A staff position in a public accounting firm.

**EDUCATION:**

J.D., December 1994
Bolt Law School, University of California, Berkeley
GPA - 3.5

B.A., History, 1989
Wabash College, Crawfordsville, IN
GPA - 3.9

**EMPLOYMENT:**

1995–2000
Price Waterhouse & Co., Indianapolis, IN
*Tax Consultant*

1992
Arnerich, Kelsey & White, Indianapolis, IN
*Legal Assistant*

1991–1995
Marion Electronics, Southport, IN
*Customer Service Representative*

1990
Carmel Township School District
Westfield Township School District
Washington Township School District
*Substitute Teacher*

**EXPERIENCE:**

Directed several research projects for major clients.
Completed tax returns and workpapers for individual partnerships and corporations.
Proficient in Microsoft Excel and Microsoft Access.

**REFERENCES:**

Available upon request.

# STEVE MYERS

| Present Address | Permanent Address |
|---|---|
| 80 Harbor Way, #35 | 27 Bridger Way |
| Seattle, WA 98195 | Bellevue, WA 98008 |
| (206) 555-9892 | (206) 555-3912 |

## OBJECTIVE

To obtain a financial position that capitalizes on my construction experience.

## EDUCATION

University of Washington, Seattle, WA
Currently pursuing Master's of Business Administration degree with a concentration in finance and marketing.
Expected Graduation: May 2001

Purdue University, West Lafayette, IN
Bachelor of Science in Civil Engineering
Graduated: May 1995

## EXPERIENCE

Granite Construction, Watsonville, CA
Summer 2000

Business Development Associate: Assisted in the preparation of bid proposals for heavy construction projects. Prepared project budgets, long-range plans, and financial analysis.

Morrison-Knudsen, Saudi Arabia
1995–1999

Cost Engineer: Prepared cost forecasts for development of offshore gas reserves. Identified potential problem areas in the construction budget and recommended solutions. Involved in the preparation of plans for construction of an oil refinery. Evaluated construction progress and workforce performance.

## ADDITIONAL INFORMATION

Traveled extensively in the Middle East.
Member, American Society of Civil Engineers.

## REFERENCES

Supplied on request.

**Cynthia T. Porter**
21 Sycamore Avenue
Chattanooga, TN 37401
615-555-4662 home
615-555-3454 cell phone

## OBJECTIVE

To obtain a position in the real estate industry.

## EXPERIENCE

Summer 2000, Associate, Real Properties, Inc., New York, NY.

>   Verified underwriter's statistical analysis of residential mortgage pools.
>   Recalculated adjustable rate mortgage payment schedules during a sample audit.

1997–1999, Analyst, Citibank, New York, NY.

>   Implemented a new system for settling LDC bank loans.
>   Performed interest calculations, position reconciliations, and interest claim receivables and payables.
>   Completed trade transactions and maintained trade database.

1995–1996, Facility Developer, Computer Accessories, Knoxville, TN.

>   Developed a software training school at an IBM specialty store.
>   Analyzed local market, designed marketing strategy, established course program, and hired teachers.

## EDUCATION

Fuqua School of Management, Durham, NC
M.B.A., Finance, May 2001

University of Tennessee, Knoxville, TN
B.B.A., May 1995

## REFERENCES

Furnished on request.

# Laura C. Rudolph

*68 East 29th Avenue, #18C*
*Philadelphia, PA 19104*
*(215) 555-7504*
*lcrudolph@xxx.net*

## Education

**Wharton School of Business,** Philadelphia, PA
M.B.A., Finance, May 2001
Investment Club, Real Estate Club, Admissions Interviewer

**University of Pennsylvania,** Philadelphia, PA
B.A., Economics, May 1987
Phi Beta Kappa, Dean's list, golf team

## Experience

**Office of Kobe Sato, H.O.R.,** Tokyo, Japan
Legislative Assistant, Summer 2001

Provided research and translation services to a member of the Liberal Democratic Party.

**Cushman and Wakefield,** Philadelphia, PA
Sales Intern, Summer 2000

Cold-called potential clients. Prepared sales presentations for brokers. Responsible for the Philadelphia metropolitan area.

**Leisure Developments,** Honolulu, HI
Assistant Project Manager, 1995–1998

Managed construction, finance, and design of three hotels. Prepared financial analyses and budgets. Handled design and construction problems.

## Personal

Proficient in Japanese.
Volunteer tutor for inner-city youths.
Drummer and singer.

**Rachel Anderson**
34 Diamond Head Way
Honolulu, HI 96813
home: (808) 555-7834
cellular: (808) 555-9876

## PROFILE

A finance and credit industry professional with over 20 years of experience in operations and branch management combined with strong retail and real property lending skills.

### Operations Management

Progressed to managerial positions through a series of merit promotions; currently Branch Operations Manager for two branches.

Effective in assuming decision-making responsibilities regarding hiring, promotions, and day-to-day operations.

### Lending

An experienced loan officer in consumer, commercial, and real estate lending with specialized knowledge of loan center production.

## EXPERIENCE

Bank of Hawaii
1990 - present

*Assistant Vice President & Branch Manager* (2000 - present) Honolulu, HI

Coordinate all aspects of branch supervision and assume direct accountability for quality operating conditions with strong emphasis on customer sales and service.

Actively participate in business development goals and branch planning, including income and expense controls.

*Assistant Vice President & Branch Manager* (1998 - 2000) Lahaina, HI

*Assistant Vice President, Senior Credit Analyst* (1997 - 1998) Honolulu, HI

Senior credit analyst of consumer loan portfolios, including unsecured, auto, and home-secured loans.

Developed and implemented consumer loan training for branch personnel, in addition to serving as representative of the Consumer Loan Center in District/Branch Manager monthly meetings.

Established loan center's regulatory compliance program, and participated in improvements to automated loan processing system for Hawaii.

*Rachel Anderson—page one of two*

*Assistant Manager, Branch Operations & Loans* (1995 - 1996) Waimea, HI

*Assistant Manager, Branch Operations & Loans* (1994 - 1995) Honolulu, HI

*Merchant Teller, Notes & Collections/Exchange (*1990 - 1993) Honolulu, HI
Various duties including operational functions of Bank of Hawaii.

## TRAINING

*Bank of Hawaii*
Credit I & II
Attended various advanced management skills workshops and seminars.

*American Banker's Association*
Regulatory Compliance

## EDUCATION

Stanford University, A.B., English, 1990

## REFERENCES

Available upon request.

**LEWIS B. PULLMAN**
325 RIVER BOULEVARD
WASHINGTON, DC 01314
(202) 555-4810 HOME
(202) 555-4354 CELLULAR

Over 25 years' experience in leading growth and turnaround companies. Solid track record in management, strategic planning, finance, and marketing. Established excellent working relationships with state and federal regulators.

## PROFESSIONAL SUMMARY

- Developed goals and strategies to turn around a troubled bank. Managed the loan department recovery team, which reduced loan delinquencies, recovered $300,000 in previously charged-off loans, and reduced non-earning assets.

- Managed turnaround for $40 million bank experiencing problems in loan portfolio, accounting, and administration. Oversaw the sale of the mortgage department.

- Spearheaded reorganization of bank operations department. Formulated new standard operating controls and communications systems.

- Led major bank conversion to new data processing system.

- Reorganized real estate loan servicing department that was experiencing difficulties.

- Took charge of opening new bank, which included sale of stock, organization, and staff training.

- Implemented loan review, wrote new loan documentation, and devised collection procedures for a bank with decreasing loan quality.

## WORK EXPERIENCE

CAPITAL BANK, Washington, DC                                     1998–2001
*President and CEO*
Formulated and implemented goals and strategies in major areas needed to improve and sustain the bank's operating performance. Directed corrective action, wrote policies, and reported on regulatory compliance concerns, which led to an improved rating.

*Lewis Pullman—page one of two*

NORTHEAST THRIFT COMPANY, Bellingham, MD          1996–1998
*President and CEO*
Developed business plan to enable bank to acquire FDIC insurance.

GREAT NORTHERN BANK, Portland, NY                 1994–1996
*President and CEO*
Implemented strategic plan that corrected accounting, administration, operations, and loan procedure problems.

PORTLAND FIRST, Portland, NY                      1990–1993
*Executive Vice President and COO*
Established loan audit and review department. Implemented business development program that substantially increased market share.

*Senior Vice President*
Spearheaded restructure and reorganization plan for $700 million banking group.
Supervised conversion to new data processing system.

## EDUCATION

University of Washington, B.S., Finance           1971

Additional coursework in management, finance, and regulatory compliance.

*Lewis Pullman—page two of two*

Shari K. Portman
861 Lake Avenue
Salt Lake City, UT 84109
Office: (801) 555-4600
Home: (801) 555-8945
E-mail: skportman@xxx.com

## CURRENT POSITION

Peat Marwick, Salt Lake City, UT, 1995–present.
*Insurance and Claims Specialist*

> Research and analyze claims in conjunction with the risk management and claims consultants. Evaluate claims procedures, third party administrators' personnel, and governmental agencies for general liability and workers' compensation claims. Research insurance and legal issues for clients. Analyze policy language, accumulate data, and prepare written reports.

## EXPERIENCE

Insurance Publishing, New York, NY, 1992–1995.
*Director of Property-Casualty Programs*

> Authored texts, examinations, and training materials for agents, underwriters, and claims representatives.
> Managed each project from development through production.

Aetna Life Insurance, Hartford, CT, 1989–1992.
*Underwriter, Rater, Field Representative, and Claims Adjuster*

## EDUCATION

Smith College, B.A., History, 1986.
Certificate in General Insurance
Associate in Risk Management

## PUBLICATIONS

*General Liability Coverage,* New York: Insurance Publishing, 1999
*Business Owners Coverage,* New York, Insurance Publishing, 1996
Ten training programs
State licensing supplements

**ARTHUR PAUL EVERETT**
**72 Lighthouse Lane**
**Coral Gables, FL**
**(305) 555-4132**

*EDUCATION*

University of South Florida, Tampa, FL
Bachelor of Science in Biology
Graduate May 2001

Summer Study: University of South Florida Marine Lab, Tampa, FL
Biological Oceanography, Summer 2000

*EXPERIENCE*

**Financial Intern** - Bank of Miami, Miami, FL, Summer 2001

Solved individual account problems for clients. Processed transfer of new stock for over one thousand client accounts after bank acquisition of Marine Banks. Standardized management reports for customer service department.

**Environmental Law Intern** - Mitchell & Keller Law Firm, Summer 1999

Assisted in the preparation of pretrial files for clients in the environmental section.

**Counselor** - Oceanlife Camp, Summer 1998

Instructed campers in scuba diving, snorkeling, lifesaving, and marine wildlife. Responsible for all campers between the ages of 13 and 18. Organized and coordinated group activities.

*SKILLS AND ACTIVITIES*

Marine Explorers Club
University of South Florida Diving and Swim Club
Proficient in library research, writing, and editing
Experienced with Microsoft Word, Microsoft Excel, website design

**Clara Bacon**
1260 Michigan Blvd., #8D
Grand Rapids, MI 49506
(616) 555-6189

OBJECTIVE

To obtain a financial management position with responsibility for supervision, operations, and profitability.

EDUCATION

B.S. in Accounting, Kalamazoo College, 1982

CAREER SUMMARY

**Northview Hospital**
October 1998 to present
Grand Rapids, MI
*Assistant to the Controller*
Prepare monthly financial statements, account reconciliations, bank analysis, and general ledger entries.

**Accountemps**
June 1997 to October 1998
Grand Rapids, MI
*Staff Accountant*
Performed accounts receivable, accounts payable, and payroll accounting functions as well as financial statement preparation for manufacturing and insurance companies.

**Union State Savings Bank**
November 1987 to June 1997
Flint, MI
*Accountant*
Responsible for general accounting procedures, daily cash management, and supervision of department personnel. Prepared the monthly and quarterly regulatory financial statements and management reports. Chaired a committee for a bankwide data processing conversion, including the evaluation of equipment, procedures, and training.

*Page one of two*

**First National Bank of Ypsilanti**
November 1982 to November 1987
Ypsilanti, MI
Responsible for financial and management reporting as well as general ledger reconciliations. Gained experience as a teller and in the bookkeeping and loan departments.

ACCOMPLISHMENTS

**Accounting Management**
Developed profit center accounting and responsibility reporting for the department heads. Participated in the implementation of the Competitive Equality Banking Act of 1995.

**Efficiency/Automation**
Automated the general ledger system to allow for company expansion and for product and responsibility center reporting. Centralized office supplies for branch offices by automating the purchasing and disbursing procedures.

**Procedure Establishment**
Improved reconciliation procedures in the accounting department. Implemented operating procedures for teller and branch balancing function and for ATM network.

*Michelle C. Trayhern*
*68 Cody Court*
*Kansas City, Missouri 78284*
*Home: (816) 555-0561*
*Cellular: (816) 555-9876*

## OBJECTIVE

Position as a business development/administration manager

## QUALIFICATIONS

Successful record of establishment, management, and staff training for effective marketing and improved sales production.

- Directed department that exceeded sales goals by 150 percent.
- Created $75 million in new business for department.
- Managed budgets totaling over $2 million.

## ACCOMPLISHMENTS

1997 - 2001      HORIZON DEPOSIT GROUP, Kansas City, MO
                 Assistant Vice President

Established marketing procedures for new loan department. Implemented nationwide home equity program.

- Sourced business, trained staff, and developed service standards.
- Created $75 million in new construction loan business.
- Developed new credit line product; launched product in marketplace.

1995 - 1997      KANSAS CITY FEDERAL BANK, Kansas City, MO
                 Business Development Manager

Created statewide mortgage loan division and managed Missouri marketing base of various banks, mortgage banks, and mortgage brokers.

- Exceeded sales goals by 80 percent.
- Established departmental policies and procedures.
- Hired and trained professional staff.

1993 - 1995      MIDWEST FINANCIAL GROUP, Kansas City, MO
                 Commercial Broker

Bundled major loans for funding and brokered loan and investment sources.

- Established Kansas marketing base.
- Developed new business techniques.
- Generated $30 million in new business.

1989 - 1993     AMERICAN FLETCHER BANK, St. Louis, MO
                Assistant Vice President

Managed major consumer credit loan portfolio. Developed and marketed bankcard accounts.

- Performed quality review for loans.
- Established lending procedures.
- Exceeded initial goals for new bankcard accounts by 50 percent.

1983 - 1989     WICHITA BANK & TRUST COMPANY, Wichita, KS
                Vice President

Managed three loan programs in the consumer credit division.

- Directed executive credit program.
- Administered $1.5 million budget.
- Hired and trained personnel in credit procedures.

EDUCATION

1979            Kansas State University, B.A., Economics

REFERENCES

Available upon request.

## EDITH BURNETT
**689 Oak Street, #12**
**Jackson, Mississippi 39217**
**(601) 555-3590 home**
**(601) 555-8193 work**

### EXPERIENCE

Over 10 years of experience in the real estate industry with emphasis on underwriting construction loans, risk analysis and profitability, and portfolio administration.

### EMPLOYMENT HISTORY

*Assistant Vice President:* Bank of Mississippi in Jackson, 1994–present

Responsible for residential and commercial construction loans.

Negotiate terms and structure with borrower.

Prepare and present financial analysis for committee approval and ensure proper loan documentation.

*Closing Officer:* International Investment Mortgage Company, New Orleans, 1991–1994

Responsible for loan documentation and closing for participator loans ranging from $30 million to $50 million.

*Account Assistant:* Merchants Bank, New Orleans, 1988–1991

Responsible for preparation of loan requests.

### EDUCATION

University of Alabama, 1988
Degree: B.S., Business Administration

DARRYL MONK
46 RIDGE DRIVE, APT. 16D
MENOMONIE, WI 54751
715/555-8765
E-MAIL: DDMONK@XXX.NET

## *EMPLOYMENT HISTORY*

**Smith Barney,** New York, NY
June 2000 to August 2000
Associate

- Analyzed multinational companies using cash flow, expected earnings, and dividend discount models as part of corporate advisory services.

- Publicized initial public offering through roadshows, strategy meetings, and client presentations.

**Wisconsin Marine Companies,** Superior, WI
July 1997 to December 1999
Marine Underwriter

- Underwrote marine risks of corporations involved in international trade.

- Analyzed commercial and economic risk of commodities shipped overseas.

- Directed and marketed $7.5 million of business capital.

- Supervised staff of three.

## *EDUCATION*

M.B.A., University of Wisconsin, 2001

B.A., Economics, Dennison University, 1997

**Thomas R. Curry**

*P.O. Box 333*
*New Haven, CT*
*(203) 555-1527 home*
*(203) 555-3434 cell*

## Objective

Financial analyst position that utilizes my analytical and technical skills.

## Education

Yale University, New Haven, CT
Major: Quantitative Economics
GPA: 3.9/4.0
Expected Graduation: May 2001

## Experience

*Financial Analyst,* Citibank
Summer 2000

Researched the creditworthiness of the financial sector in Brazil, Argentina, and Chile. Conducted an industry study on Brazilian mining to predict current growth trends.

*Financial Intern,* Bank of Charleston
Summer 1999

Analyzed investors' risk capacities and recommended appropriate portfolio strategies. Developed a cost-effective plan for maintaining client base.

*Intern,* Bank of the South
Summer 1998

Assisted in the preparation of reports on pension and retirement fund management. This involved analyzing financial statements, synthesizing relevant data, and producing the report.

*Tutor,* Youth Education
Summer 1997

Tutored students entering their senior year in high school in calculus and economics.

## Additional Information

Member, Yale Ski Team.
Big Brother.
Proficient in WordPerfect, Microsoft Excel, and Harvard Graphics.

## John S. Kelsey

Current Address:
865 Olympic Drive, #10F
Los Angeles, CA 90089

Permanent Address:
4689 Beach Street
La Jolla, CA 92093

Cellular Phone: (310) 555-4579

**EDUCATION:**

University of Southern California
Los Angeles, CA
B.A., Economics/History anticipated Winter 2001

**VARSITY ATHLETICS**

Cross Country, 2001 Captain
Track and Field, Qualified for 2001 Pac 10
Conference Championships in 10,000 meters

**EXPERIENCE:**

Summer 2001: California Mortgage Insurance Company
Los Angeles, CA
*Loan Administrator:* Answered customer demands for information and other assistance. Processed loans and organized loan files. Served as liaison between home office and field office.

Summer 2000 and Fall 2001: Merrill Lynch
Los Angeles, CA
*Analyst:* Researched stocks and mutual funds.
Performed hypothetical analyses on computer. Assisted brokers with their daily operations.

Summer 1999: The Highland Group
Los Angeles, CA
*Intern:* Screened and developed government proposals for management consulting client. Participated in the development of a strategic plan for The Highland Group.

**RELEVANT SKILLS:**

Network Technician: expertise in Microsoft Systems Management Server 2.0, NT 4.0, NT workstation and NT servers.
Fluent in American Sign Language.

Grace Delaney
1000 Chestnut Street
San Francisco, CA 94117
(415) 555-9080 home
(415) 555-5687 cell

## OBJECTIVE

Financial management position with personal and professional growth potential.

## PROFESSIONAL EXPERIENCE

### Coopers & Lybrand (1995 to present)

I have been employed by Coopers & Lybrand for over five years. As an audit supervisor, I am responsible for all facets of audit and non-audit engagements including planning, budgeting, report preparation, and supervision of senior and staff accountants. I have client service responsibilities for public and privately held companies in the retail food service, construction, and manufacturing industries.

Specific experience and achievements with Coopers & Lybrand include:

Involvement in the initial public stock offerings for five clients which included discussions with and reporting to the Securities and Exchange Commission.

Supervision of services for a developmental stage steel mill which entailed becoming familiar with complex financing arrangements.

Experience in the use of microcomputers and the input and output data from all sizes of EDP shops.

Performance of special litigation support procedures.

Consultation in the sale of client business which included contacting potential buyers.

## PROFESSIONAL ORGANIZATIONS

American Institute of Certified Public Accountants, California
Association of Certified Public Accountants

## EDUCATION

Bachelor of Science in Business Administration
Major in Accounting
University of San Francisco, 1995

## REFERENCES

Furnished upon request.

## Warren L. Peabody

385 East 90th Street, #4G
New York, NY 10026
(212) 555-4967 home
(212) 555-8790 cell

**OBJECTIVE**  A financial management position with a metropolitan museum.

**EXPERIENCE**

Summer 2000  The Smithsonian, Washington, DC
*Financial Intern*

Redesigned budget projection system. Evaluated the efficiency of museum's operations. Created database of capital projects for accurate reporting and cash flow projections.

1997–1998  Kidder Peabody & Co., New York, NY
*Financial Analyst*

Worked on debt, equity, mergers and acquisition, and private placements for food industry companies. Derived cash flow and sensitivity analysis models. Interviewed prospective analysts.

Summer 1996  Trade Exhibitions in Germany, New York, NY
*Trade Show Representative*

Assisted in the planning, budgeting, and promoting of consumer goods trade shows in Germany.

**EDUCATION**

New York University Business School, New York, NY
M.B.A., 2000

Columbia University, New York, NY
B.A., Economics, 1996

**RICHARD DEAN**
**145 King Court**
**Cincinnati, Ohio 45228**
**(513) 555-4961**

## EMPLOYMENT HISTORY

### OHIO REAL ESTATE ASSOCIATES
Cincinnati, Ohio

Chief Financial Officer and Treasurer
1998–present
- Managed and reorganized the corporate finance, administration, and personnel functions.
- Developed and maintained banking relationships with Bank One, American Fletcher, Chemical Bank, Continental Bank, and Citibank.
- Implemented executive benefits and deferred compensation plans.
- Designed an information system to track tax planning issues.

Senior Vice President of Asset Services
1991–1998
- Created the Asset Services division consisting of property and asset management, financial services, risk management, and real estate finance.
- Negotiated contracts with developers, lessees, and lenders that increased investor returns and property values.
- Managed the working capital funds which included reinvestment of individual property funds.

Controller
1990–1991
- Developed the financial services function.

### DELOITTE & TOUCHE
Omaha, Nebraska

Senior Accountant
1987–1990

## EDUCATION

University of Nebraska, B.S., Accounting

## Karen Monroe
495 Garden Avenue, #16
Manhattan, KS 66506
(913) 555-2101

### EDUCATION

Kansas State University, Manhattan, KS
B.S., December 2000
Major: Economics
Concentration: Accounting
Overall GPA: 3.9 on a 4.0 scale

### EMPLOYMENT

*Manager/Waitress*
Pizza Hut Restaurant, September 1999–present
Assist in opening, setting up the books, and designing work stations. Perform book-keeping function. Supervise and train waitstaff.

*Student Assistant*
Kansas State University, December 1999–August 2000
Graded homework and papers, proctored exams, and tutored students in the statistics department.

*Senior Project*
Kansas State University, April 2000–August 2000
Analyzed and researched audit, tax, and accounting issues

### HONORS AND ACTIVITIES

Dean's list
Kansas State Accounting Club
Phi Beta Kappa Honor Society

LLOYD K. EVANS
3600 HAWTHORNE
MINNEAPOLIS, MN 55455
(612) 555-4916

## EXPERIENCE

April 1998–Present
**Marquette National Bank**
*Supervisory Assistant*
Responsible for consumer, commercial, and construction support which includes personnel supervision, insurance follow-up, balancing, construction draws, escrow instructions, and documentation.

December 1995–February 1998
**Bank of St. Cloud**
*Commercial Note Department Supervisor*
Responsible for supervision of all aspects pertinent to commercial and consumer loans. Duties included processing payments, maintaining zero-accrual loans, and following up on loans.

January 1992–November 1995
**First Bank of St. Cloud**
*Loan Department Supervisor*
Responsible for supervising personnel, maintaining loans, and preparing documents. Also responsible for supervision of office functions which included bookkeeping, new accounts, and teller line.

January 1988–December 1992
**United Bank of Duluth**
*Operations Officer*
Responsible for bank operations, all personnel, and the note department. Prepared and submitted payroll and monthly operations reports.

## EDUCATION

American Institute of Banking, M.B.A.
December 1987

Hennepin Community College, Bachelor's Degree in Accounting
June 1987

## MARGARET FONG

*16201 Blossom Hill Road*
*San Jose, CA 95008*
*(408) 555-2985 cell phone*
*(408) 555-8923 home phone*

### SUMMARY

Experienced financial lending professional with strong analytical skills in all areas of banking. Background in commercial and construction lending, branch management, and new business development.

### EXPERIENCE

December 1997–Present
COMMUNITY BANK OF LOS GATOS, Los Gatos, California
*Vice President/Regional Manager*

- Manage portfolio of new and existing commercial loans.
- Negotiate and structure loans for financial feasibility, industry analysis, and collateral evaluation.
- Implemented new construction lending department.
- Improved credit quality of substandard loan portfolio.
- Established 80 new commercial accounts during fiscal year 2000 in new Saratoga branch.

October 1994–November 1997
SANTA CLARA BANK, Santa Clara, California
*Vice President/Manager*

- Directed a $20 million branch; supervised all operations, new business development, and lending.
- Developed branch into a profitable entity in four years.
- Increased total deposits 30 percent annually.
- Increased commercial loan portfolio 400 percent in three years.

July 1992–October 1994
FIRST NATIONAL BANK, San Jose, California
*Branch Manager*

- Consistently met or exceeded branch goals and profit projections.

### EDUCATION

San Jose State University, B.S. in marketing

### COMMUNITY SERVICES

Chamber of Commerce, Los Gatos
Finance Committee, Los Gatos Methodist Church
City of Los Gatos Business Development Committee

CHET ROGERS
_____

*865 Veteran Street, #12C*
*Los Angeles, California 90024*
*home: (310) 555-8283*
*cellular: (213) 555-1236*

OBJECTIVE:       Challenging position as a tax accountant.

EDUCATION:       Master of Business Administration, March 1999.
                 Anderson Graduate School of Management at University of California–
                 Los Angeles. GPA: 3.9, Dean's list.

                 Marketing and Sales Management Diploma, July 1995.
                 Pacific Institute of Management, Kyoto, Japan.

                 Bachelor of Science in Mechanical Engineering, June 1989.
                 University of California at Davis.

EXPERIENCE:      Huntington Tax, Inc., San Francisco, California. *Tax Analyst Intern*
                 Advise tax accountants on input requirements for computerized indi-
                 vidual, partnership, and corporation tax returns. Debug tax return
                 computer programs. (March 1999 - present)

                 Anderson Graduate School of Management at University of California–
                 Los Angeles. *Teaching Assistant*
                 Assisted students in finance, macroeconomics, and forecasting. Acted
                 as a technical instructor in the computer center.
                 (January 1998 - March 1999)

                 General Motors Taiwan, Ltd., Taipei, Taiwan. *Senior Spare Parts
                 Executive*
                 Developed spare parts network. Prepared recommendation lists, priced
                 parts for local markets, ordered parts, and computerized systems.
                 Trained dealer personnel.
                 (January 1997 - July 1997)

                 Singapore Honda, Singapore. *Parts Executive*
                 Established spare parts dealerships. Served as liaison between Honda
                 and the government of Singapore on import policy and procedure.
                 (August 1995 - December 1996)

                 Thailand Engineering Company, Bangkok, Thailand. *Parts Executive*
                 Prepared inventory reduction programs for fleet operators and insti-
                 tutional customers. Designed retail parts center, regional warehouse,
                 and implemented distribution system.
                 (July 1991 - July 1994)

REFERENCES:      Furnished on request.

## ARTHUR K. MONTGOMERY

*614 Camelback Road*
*Phoenix, AZ 85021*
*(602) 555-2311 home*
*(602) 555-3785 cellular/mobile*
*E-mail: akmontgomery@xxx.net*

## CAREER OBJECTIVE

A position where my acquired financial expertise will enhance the organization.

## EXPERIENCE

*The State Bank of Phoenix, AZ—11/94 to present*
*Senior Vice President*

Monitor all lending functions. Responsible for daily bank operations and supervising a staff of five.

*Union Bank, Denver, CO—1/92 to 10/94*
*President*

Responsible for the financial and business management of bank operations.

*Community Bank, Boulder, CO—9/88 to 12/91*
*President*

*Valley Hospital, Boulder, CO—5/87 to 8/88*
*Credit Officer*

*The Bank of Nevada, Reno, NV—1/84 to 4/87*
*Assistant Vice President*

Advanced through the positions of Collection Supervisor and Branch Manager for Installment Loan Center, Assistant Manager for Credit Card Division, and Commercial Loan Officer to become Assistant Vice President.

*Regional Loan Company, Las Vegas, NV—9/81 to 12/83*
*Manager*

## EDUCATION

Arizona Graduate School of Banking, Phoenix, AZ, 1981

University of California at San Diego, 1978

REGINA FORD

*1532 Walnut Street*
*Sacramento, CA 95819*
*(916) 555-3663 home*
*(916) 555-3474 cellular*

OBJECTIVE

A supervisory position that utilizes my experience and skills to generate staff effectiveness, enhance productivity, and meet organizational goals.

SUMMARY OF QUALIFICATIONS

- Sixteen years of experience in retail banking and five years in operations.
- Skilled at team building, creative problem solving, and technical training.
- Communicate well with senior management, staff, and customers.

ANALYSIS OF EXPERIENCE

**Supervision**

- Monitored daily workload.
- Hired and trained staff.
- Established policies for handling customer complaints to promote quality service and quick resolution.
- Prepared monthly management reports.
- Developed employee incentive program.
- Introduced ideas that reduced expenses by 25 percent.

**Customer Service**

- Directed staff of 10 customer service representatives.
- Settled payment disputes.
- Answered almost 300 calls and letters daily.
- Redesigned job functions to improve quality control standards.
- Cross-trained staff in several positions to cover for vacations and absences.

**Accounting**

- Reconciled outstanding items on bank statements.
- Cleared and reconciled bank advances.
- Established new depository account procedures.

*page one of two*

*WORK EXPERIENCE*

**Customer Service Supervisor**
First National Bank
Sacramento, CA
1996–2001

**Branch Service Manager**
Wells Fargo
Modesto, CA
1990–1996

**Operations Supervisor**
Wells Fargo
Stockton, CA
1984–1990

*EDUCATION*

California State University, Sacramento
Business Management degree, 1984
Several American Institute of Banking courses

*PERSONAL INTERESTS*

Bowling, hiking, softball, and reading

# CHERYL LAMBERT

**20317 FOUNTAIN ROAD**
**DALLAS, TEXAS 75230**
**(214) 555-3658 HOME**
**(212) 555-8989 CELLULAR**

## Professional Experience

**Vice President and Cashier**
*Southwest Bank, Dallas, Texas*
July 1994–present

> Supervise the administration of the operations and personnel functions. Responsible for accounting, budgeting, purchasing, and bank development. Manage the preparation of all financial reports for the bank and regulatory agencies.

**Bank Consultant**
*Lambert Consulting, Dallas, Texas*
January 1992–June 1994

> Advised groups that were creating new banks in the Dallas-Fort Worth area. This included preparing financial reports, assisting in filing with regulatory agencies, issuing stock, ordering supplies, and installing information systems.

**Vice President and Cashier**
*Dallas National Bank, Dallas, Texas*
August 1989–December 1991

> Supervised the administration of operations and personnel functions. Responsible for accounting, budgeting, investing, and purchasing. Managed the preparation of all financial reports for the bank and regulatory agencies. Participated in the development of a new loan program.

**Vice President and Cashier**
*First Bank of Houston, Houston, Texas*
September 1984–July 1989

> Directed the organization of a new bank in the Post Oak area that included hiring and training staff, installing systems, and purchasing the necessary equipment. After the opening, assumed responsibility for daily bank administration. Supervised accounting, operation, personnel, investment, and financial report preparation functions.

*C. Lambert—page one of two*

Professional Experience, continued

---

**Assistant Vice President and Manager**
*Bank of Commerce, Houston, Texas*
March 1981–April 1984

**Assistant Cashier and Loan Officer**
*Consolidated Bank, Houston, Texas*
September 1973–January 1981

**Teller**
*BankWest, Houston, Texas*
June 1971–August 1973

Education

---

Texas A & M University, B.B.A., Accounting, 1971
Various American Institute of Banking courses completed

**References will be furnished on request.**

## LORENZO FREITAS

2986 Via Corte Madera
Miami, FL 33054
(305) 555-7296 (Home)
(305) 555-1812 (Work)

## EMPLOYMENT

### SHORELINE PROPERTIES
1999–present
Consultant and Owner

Responsibilities:
Consult banks and individuals on commercial and government-assisted loan placement as well as real estate acquisition, disposition, and development.

### FLORIDA EQUITIES
1996–1999
Chief Operating Officer

Responsibilities:
Managed day-to-day operations of this real estate development and management firm. Florida Equities specializes in commercial office buildings and residential development.

### FIRST NATIONAL BANK OF MIAMI
1980–1996
Chief Financial Officer (1991–1996)

Responsibilities:

*Investments*
Chairman of Funds Management Committee that determined type, size, maturity, and mix of all investments. Set loan and deposit rates weekly. In charge of public funds, repurchase agreements, and lease financing.

*Loans*
Managed a commercial, real estate, and consumer loan portfolio of over $25 million.

*Marketing*
Supervised this department which included establishing budgets and determining advertising and marketing programs.

*Personnel*
Supervised this department which included defining staff requirements, job classifications, and salary levels. Coadministrator of profit sharing and benefit retirement plans.

*Branch Administration*
Responsible for loans, operations, personnel, and branch building development.

*page one of two*

Comptroller (1987–1991)

Responsibilities:

Accounting, operations, fund management, budget development, and cost controls.

Auditor (1984–1987)

Assistant Cashier (1983)

Transit Manager (1980–1982)

## EDUCATION

B.S., Finance, University of Florida, 1980
Graduate School of Banking, University of North Carolina, Chapel Hill, 1982
Certificates from School for Bank Auditors, School of Banking, School of Bank Investments, and Commercial Lending School

## ORGANIZATIONS

Member, Florida Bankers Association
Appointed to the Bank Investment and Trust Committee
Miami Chamber of Commerce
Member, Financial Executives Institute

**Matthew L. Scott**
**590 La Honda**
**Palo Alto, CA 94307**
**415-555-7359**

## BUSINESS EXPERIENCE

**1993–present**          **Hewlett Packard, Inc.**

*Corporate Treasurer (9/94–present)*
Responsible for cash management, foreign exchange, investing, bank relations, financing activities, insurance and risk management, and taxes.
Also responsible for export licensing, international order processing, and international and domestic distribution.

*Assistant Treasurer (1/93–8/94)*
Responsible for taxes, leasing, and special financing projects.

**1990–1992**          **General Instruments**

*Director, Corporate Taxes*
Responsible for all tax matters.

**1987–1989**          **Amdahl Corporation**

*Manager, Domestic Taxes*
Responsible for all corporate tax matters, which included tax planning and research.

**1983–1986**          **Equitable Life Assurance Society**

*Assistant Tax Manager (9/85–11/86)*
Created department to handle all tax research, planning, and audits.

*Assistant East Coast Tax Manager (3/83–8/85)*
Supervised tax compliance.
Performed tax research and planning.
Handled tax audits.

**1980–1982**          **Lowell Properties**

*Assistant Tax Manager*
Responsible for tax compliance, audits, and planning.

**1977–1979**          **Price Waterhouse**

*Senior Tax Accountant*
Performed tax planning, research, and compliance work.

## EDUCATION

M.B.A., University of Chicago, 1977

B.A., Economics, Boston College, 1975

PAULA G. URBELZ
*438 Shoreline Drive, #6*
*Miami, FL 33199*
*(305) 555-4613*

## EDUCATION

Loyola University of Chicago
J.D., December 1997
GPA: 3.5
Relevant Courses: Personal Tax, Corporate Tax, Advanced Corporations, Foreign Income/Transactions Tax, Business Planning, and Advanced Personal Tax

Hastings Law School, San Francisco, CA
Summer 1997
International Tax Course

Florida State University, Tallahassee, FL
Bachelor of Science, Accounting, June 1995

## SUMMARY OF EXPERIENCE

LAW CLERK, July 1996–December 1996
Law Offices of Jorge Escondido, Esq.
Researched legal issues in taxation.
Assisted in discovery process.
Drafted various documents including motions, trial briefs, interrogatories, and appellate briefs.

STUDENT ASSISTANT, April 1995–June 1995
Florida State University
Music Department
Researched musical works for the music library.

PBX OPERATOR, May 1994–October 1994
Hilton Hotels
Operated hotel's PBX system.
Managed main business lobby.
Performed administrative support work.

## ADDITIONAL INFORMATION

Certified in LEXIS and WESTLAW.
Speak fluent Spanish.

MARTIN CHANG
964 NORTH TENTH ST.
SPRINGFIELD, IL 62713
(217) 555-5240

## *PROFESSIONAL OBJECTIVE*

A financial position with a dynamic company engaged in the manufacture of steel products.

## *WORK EXPERIENCE*

*Senior Financial Analyst at the Illinois Department of Commerce,* Springfield, IL, June 1998–present

   Represented the State of Illinois in its economic development efforts targeted toward the steel, appliance, and automotive industries.

   Attracted new capital investment and job creation.

   Proposed, negotiated, and delivered state financial incentive packages.

   Trained new financial analysts.

*Staff Assistant at Illinois Employment Development Commission,* Springfield, IL, June 1996–June 1998

   Promoted and implemented the Illinois Loan Guarantee program.

   Participated in establishing the export finance committee to provide direct loans and U.S. Export-Import Bank insurance to Illinois exporters.

*Loan Committee Member at the New Development Corporation,* Chicago, IL, January 1994–May 1996

   Reviewed applications from Illinois businesses and banks for loans through the Small Business Administration.

   Prepared loan recommendations for committee discussion.

## *EDUCATION*

Northwestern University, Evanston, Illinois
Bachelor of Arts in Economics - May 1993
Grade Point Average - 3.4/4.0

*Chang, page 1 of 2*

Coursework focused on business management, history, and political science.

First National Bank of Chicago, IL
Analysis of Commercial Credit, April–June 1986

Coursework concentrated on analysis of financial statements within different industries, evaluation of business management, and loan structuring to meet financing needs of corporate clients.

*REFERENCES AVAILABLE UPON REQUEST*

PATRICK TRILLING
200 COPPER CANYON
LOS ANGELES, CA 90024
(310) 555-5620

## OBJECTIVE

To obtain a management position in the finance arena.

## EXPERIENCE SUMMARY

Over fifteen years of progressive experience in investments and funds management developing and refining the following skills:

- Leadership/Personnel Management
- Investment Portfolio Management
- Cash Asset Management
- Funds Acquisition
- Investment Operations Management

## ACHIEVEMENTS

- Merged and transferred affiliate bank investment accounting system to a computer-based system at Wells Fargo Bank.
- Streamlined affiliate bank security safekeeping.
- Designed cash management model that enabled the user to effectively manage the daily cash positions of customers and to create the required accounting entries.
- Hired and trained personnel to operate the investment accounting system and cash management model.
- Conceived, developed, and implemented a new check-processing product.

## PROFESSIONAL EXPERIENCE

1982 - 2000
**Wells Fargo Bank,** Los Angeles, CA
*Manager–Funds Management and Check Float* (1996 - 2000)
Responsible for the following:

- Bank investment operations
- Short-term investment and funds acquisition programs
- Electronic funds transfer operations
- Funds due to and from other banks
- Check float analysis

*P. Trilling – page one of two*

*Manager - Bank Investments* (1992 - 1996)
Responsible for the following:

- Implementation of investment strategies
- Investment accounting and operations
- Funds due to and from other banks

*Manager - Investment Operations* (1989 - 1992)
Responsible for the following:

- Funds due to and from other banks
- Federal Reserve wire transfer operations

*Manager - Wire Transfer Group* (1986 - 1989)
Responsible for the following:

- Management of bank's daily cash position
- Directing work flow of wire transfer clerks

*Employee - Auditing Department* (1982 - 1985)

- Performed audits of bank departments

## EDUCATION

M.B.A., Anderson Graduate School of Management, University of California, Riverside, 1982
B.S. in Accounting, University of California, Los Angeles, 1980

### REFERENCES AVAILABLE UPON REQUEST

## THEODORE L. CRAIG, JR.

**Permanent Address**
**89 Dow Boulevard, #7C**
**Wilmington, DE 19808**
**(302) 555-8123**

## OBJECTIVE

A position with a major accounting firm in the area of taxation.

## EDUCATION

Johns Hopkins University, Baltimore, MD.
Bachelor of Science in Accounting, August 1992.

## EXPERIENCE

**Malaysia Rubber Company,** Kuala Lumpur, Malaysia. Responsible for the accounting function to the U.S. parent company, overseas purchasing, and contract negotiations. 2000–present.

**Accountancy Corporation,** Wilmington, DE. Performed audits of small businesses and management companies. 1996–2000.

**Louis P. Morgan,** CPA, PC, Wilmington, DE. Compiled and reviewed clients' financial statements. Performed litigation support and investment analysis. 1992–1995.

**Burkhart Investments,** Wilmington, DE. Licensed real estate agent. Involved in the syndication of commercial properties. June 1991–August 1991.

## ACTIVITIES

Waterskiing, exercising, and scuba diving

Board of Directors, Revere Homeowners Association

## CAROL GABLE

P.O. Box 864
Northampton, MA 01063
(413) 555-2661

### EDUCATION
Bachelor of Arts degree in Economics, May 2001
Smith College, Northampton, MA

### EMPLOYMENT
September 1998–present
*Aerobics Instructor*
Nautilus Fitness Centers, Amherst, MA
- Teach aerobics classes.
- Provide nutritional and weight loss suggestions.

Summer 2000
*Research Assistant*
Economic Development Committee, State of New Jersey, Trenton, NJ
- Researched economic topics to be included in policy statements.
- Prepared economic development background reports for the governor.
- Wrote policy statements.

Summer 1999
*Sales Representative*
Ocean Boat Rental, Atlantic City, NJ
- Created and implemented a new marketing strategy.
- Prepared revenue and expense reports.
- Trained sales personnel.

Summer 1998
*Assistant Account Representative*
Kaiser Medical, New Brunswick, NJ
- Performed billing and collection services for five group medical practices.
- Posted payments to appropriate accounts.
- Filed private insurance claims and workers compensation.

### ACTIVITIES
Captain, Smith field hockey team.
Photography Editor, Smith Magazine.

### REFERENCES
Available upon request.

## RANDALL HARDING

4829 Post Street
Philadelphia, PA 19103
(215) 555-1236

## WORK EXPERIENCE

PHILADELPHIA BANK OF COMMERCE
Philadelphia, PA

*Vice President, Commercial Loan Officer* (1998–present)
Analyze credit and make appropriate recommendations for new and existing commercial loan customers. Maintain and service commercial loan accounts.

VANGUARD SECURITIES
Philadelphia, PA

*Assistant Treasurer* (1997–1998)
Maintained and developed banking relationships. Monitored foreign currency exposures and developed hedging strategies for European subsidiary. Prepared cash flow projections on monthly, quarterly, and annual basis.

FIDELITY BANK
Philadelphia, PA

*Vice President, Marketing* (1993–1996)
*Vice President, Lending* (1991–1993)
Directed suburban offices in creating new business with middle market importing and exporting companies. Managed foreign trade loan portfolio. Direct line responsibility for several key clients and for new business development.

THE BANK OF PHILADELPHIA
Philadelphia, PA

*Vice President, Senior Lending Officer* (1989–1991)
Maintained and expanded existing customer relationships, developed new loan and deposit customers, and made loan approvals.

*Page one of two*

FIRST FEDERAL BANK
Baltimore, MD

*Vice President, International Banking - Europe* (1985–1989)
*Vice President, International Banking - Global* (1980–1985)
*Assistant Vice President, International Banking* (1978–1980)
*Senior Loan Examiner* (1976–1978)

Managed asset quality of $900 million European loan portfolio. Recommended loan requests within guidelines of return on assets, geographic marketing goals, and credit quality. Worked closely with the newly established regional branch office in Rome, Italy. Evaluated economic, social, and political environment of host country.

Managed asset quality of the international loan portfolio through growth period as assets increased by 300 percent to $2 billion.

Evaluated asset quality in domestic, corporate, and international loan portfolios.

## EDUCATION

B.A., Banking and Finance, 1968
Rutgers University, New Brunswick, NJ

## REFERENCES

Professional and personal references available upon request.

ROBIN J. LAWFORD

*68 Lake Street*
*Ann Arbor, MI 48109*
*(313) 555-7426 home*
*(313) 555-2242 cell*

## OBJECTIVE

Position in investment banking.

## PROFESSIONAL EXPERIENCE

Summer 2000
**Associate—Investment Banking, Morgan Stanley, Chicago, IL**

- Analyzed debt, equity, and derivative products for telecommunications clients.
- Worked on merger and acquisition presentation for a European client.
- Assisted in due diligence for a major industrial company's IPO.

1996–1999
**Analyst—Planning and Analysis, Cygnet Insurance Company, Paris, France**

- Drafted annual business plans and revenue and profit projections.
- Analyzed variances from fiscal plan.
- Prepared monthly financial statements for internal use.
- Improved outdated MIS mainframe application.

## EDUCATION

University of Michigan School of Business
M.B.A., Finance and Communications, 2001
Member of the International Business Club and the Women in Banking Association

Dartmouth University
B.A., English, 1996

The Sorbonne, Paris, France
Exchange Program, 1994

## ADDITIONAL INFORMATION

Fluent in French and German
Traveled extensively in Europe
Enjoy painting, water polo, and tennis

**Iris K. McKenna**
**50 River Lane**
**Manchester, NH 03104**
**(603) 555-8916**
**E-mail: ikmckenna@xxx.net**

## EXPERIENCE:

SELF-EMPLOYED, Manchester, NH

1995–present
Serve as part-time controller to several small- to medium-sized firms. Prepare corporate financial statements and tax returns. Develop cash flow and business projections for loan applications.

KEVIN R. SLOAN, Springfield, MA

1993–1995
Implemented quality control standards and human resource policies and procedures. Responsible for peer reviews, performance accomplishments, and audit assignments.

D.L. RUSH ASSOCIATES, Dallas, TX

1989–1993
Developed in-house electronic data processing audit function. Responsible for audit engagements and opening of new office in Fort Worth. Served as personnel recruiting coordinator.

PEAT MARWICK & CO., Dallas, TX

1981–1989
Advanced from staff accountant to audit manager responsible for all aspects of client service.

## EDUCATION:

M.B.A., Finance, University of Texas, Austin, TX, 1989
B.S., Economics, Rice University, Houston, TX, 1981

## PROFESSIONAL ACCREDITATION:

Certified Public Accountant in New Hampshire, Massachusetts, and Texas

## REFERENCES:

Available upon request.

## G. PERRY LAWRENCE

**250 Oak Street**                                              **(312) 555-8749 home**
**Chicago, IL 60616**                                           **(312) 555-0053 cellular**

## PROFESSIONAL EXPERIENCE

October 1999–October 2001     COOLING INTERNATIONAL               Chicago, IL
*Executive Vice President, Chief Operations and Financial Officer*
Founding principal of a venture company that has developed a proprietary line of air conditioning equipment for residential applications. The units are manufactured in Taiwan and wholesaled through a distributor in Europe and the United States. Responsibilities included corporate operations and staff functions, obtaining outside financing, maintaining distributor relationships, product development, manufacturing, and sales.

June 1995–September 1999     CLAUDE, INC.                         Concord, NH
*Executive Vice President, Chief Operating Officer*
Ran the day-to-day operations of this designer, manufacturer, and wholesaler of men's shoes. Oversaw the various corporate departments. Supervised 20 factories in Mexico, Argentina, and Korea to ensure consistent high quality. Coordinated the product design and nationwide sales efforts with production operations. Performed investor relations function. Raised additional equity funding, arranged for long-term debt reduction, and implemented a leveraged buyout.

May 1992–June 1995          HAROLD LEARNER AFFILIATES              Chicago, IL
*Vice President, Operations and Financial Analysis*
Responsible for planning, budgeting, control, and operations analysis for the various operating entities: a group of diversified companies in the manufacturing, retail, fast food, construction, and mining industries. Focused primarily on operations analysis, troubleshooting, and general management assistance to on-site managers to enhance profitability.

July 1986–May 1991          CARMICHAEL INTERNATIONAL               Detroit, MI
*Manager, Business Planning and Analysis*
Functioned as advisor and strategist for the world truck group. Responsible for operational planning, budgeting and reporting, resource allocation, competitive analysis, and market planning.

June 1984–July 1986         GENERAL MOTORS COMPANY                 Lansing, MI
*Senior Financial Analyst*
Participated in budgeting, forecasting, reporting, and analysis of operations. Completed assignments in budgeting, cost, and financial analysis departments.

## EDUCATION

1982–1984                   NORTHWESTERN UNIVERSITY                Evanston, IL
Kellogg School of Management
M.B.A. in Finance and Marketing

1977–1982                   UNIVERSITY OF ILLINOIS                 Urbana, IL
B.S. in Civil Engineering

**HENRY M. GRAVES**

Home
268 Eden Place
Philadelphia, PA 19104
(215) 555-3256

Office
300 Front Street
Philadelphia, PA 19104
(215) 555-9000

### Experience

Craig H. Mellon & Co., Philadelphia, PA
    Manager, 1994–present
    Senior Accountant, 1991–1994
    Staff Accountant, 1989–1991

Responsible for completion of audits, SEC reporting, preparation of financial statements and tax returns, time and cost budgeting, staff supervision, and performance evaluation. Instructed personnel at various seminars regarding accounting, auditing, and taxation matters. Served on wide variety of consulting assignments including budgeting and profit planning, employee benefits analysis, and profitability studies.

### Education

University of Pennsylvania, Philadelphia, PA
Bachelor of Science, cum laude, in Business Administration with major in accounting, May 1988.

### Professional Affiliations

American Institute of Certified Public Accountants
Pennsylvania CPA Society

### Civic Activities

First Church of Philadelphia
    Deacon, 1987–present
    Stewardship Committee Chairman, 2000–2001 during construction of major facility addition. Responsible for securing project financing.

Alzheimer's Association, Philadelphia Area Chapter
    Treasurer, Chairman of Finance Committee, 1997–present. Responsible for preparation of budgets and all financial reports.

Big Brothers of Greater Philadelphia
    Big Brother, 1989–present

## MARTHA M. KELLY

*12391 Elm Court*
*Toledo, Ohio 43606*
*(419) 555-1301*

*OBJECTIVE*

Management position in audit, operations, and related fields.

*SUMMARY OF QUALIFICATIONS*

Fifteen years of internal audit experience.
Three years of operations experience.
Supervised staff of 15.
Assisted with consolidation of loan processing for an affiliate bank.

*PROFESSIONAL EXPERIENCE*

### BUDGET/ANALYSIS AND EVALUATION

Analyzed branch and departmental operating procedures.
Evaluated the auditing results.
Estimated and analyzed the operations budget for over three years.

### COMMUNICATIONS AND INTERPERSONAL

Questioned auditees on operating and control procedures.
Wrote audit reports and suggested action memos.
Created written audit and operating procedures.
Conducted merit reviews.
Interviewed prospective employees.

### OFFICE MANAGEMENT/SUPERVISION

Reorganized floor plan to improve workflow efficiency.
Made departmental policy decisions.
Chaired staff meetings to inform subordinates of changes, listened to their concerns, and assisted in problem resolution.
Responsible for general ledger and system reconcilements.

*Martha M. Kelly, page 1 of 2*

## EMPLOYMENT HISTORY

Held the following positions at the First National Bank, Toledo, OH.

| | |
|---|---|
| Senior Banking Officer | 5/95 to 1/00 |
| Senior Auditor | 12/92 to 5/95 |
| Auditor | 12/90 to 12/92 |
| Assistant Auditor | 5/88 to 12/90 |
| Audit Clerk | 9/86 to 5/88 |

## EDUCATION AND TRAINING

Cornell University, Ithaca, NY
Major: Accounting
Graduated: August 1986

University of Toledo, Toledo, OH
Major: Accounting
Completed approximately 75 hours

Chartered Bank Auditor Program
Completed three of four parts

# IRIS FAN

**239 Three Lakes Drive
Sheboygan, WI 53084
(414) 555-1293**

## BUSINESS EXPERIENCE

Summer 2000—*Financial Analyst,* United Airlines, Chicago, IL

- Analyzed profitability and future revenue opportunities of frequent flyer program.
- Developed strategies that are anticipated to result in savings of $15 million.

1995 to 1999—*Account Executive,* Thompson Advertisers, New York, NY

- Formulated and implemented advertising programs for a major consumer products company.
- Managed a budget of $20 million and supervised a staff of four
- Developed business-building concept for an established product line resulting in a 10 percent increase in market share.

Summer 1994—*Brand Assistant,* Procter & Gamble, Cincinnati, OH

- Conducted competitive analysis for new product introduction.
- Tested new product concept and evaluated launch plan.
- Analyzed brand performance and developed sales conference presentation.

## EDUCATION

Sloan School of Management
M.B.A., Finance and Marketing
June 2001

University of Ohio
B.S., Finance
1995

**CHRISTOPHER LAI**

**Campus Address:**
P.O. Box 986
Evanston, IL 60043
(847) 555-7675

**Permanent Address:**
4250 Quincy Street
Rockford, IL 61108
(312) 555-3751

## EDUCATION

Northwestern University
B.S. in Business Administration—December 2001. Accounting Emphasis
Grade Point Average – 3.7
Academic Honors: Dean's list, Honor Student Society, Scholarship Award from the Illinois Society of Certified Public Accountants

## WORK EXPERIENCE

*Office Assistant*, Daryl Lawton, CPA, Chicago, IL. June 2000 to present.
Limited responsibilities in preparation of individual, partnership, and corporation federal and state tax returns; financial statements; and payroll accounting.
Communicated with clients and associated lawyers.

*Payroll Clerk*, Princeton Sewing, Inc., Chicago, IL. January 1999 to May 2000.
Handled employee payroll from processing of employee computer time records to the generation of W-2 forms.

*Billings Systems Operator for Trauma Division*, Cook County Hospital, Chicago, IL. March 1996 to December 1997.
Operated and maintained customized system for billing and receipt of payments from hospital patients.
Generated monthly activity reports.

## SKILLS AND ACTIVITIES

Member, Asian Business Alliance
Volunteer Income Tax Assistant
Writing tutor for foreign students
Fluent in Chinese

**RONALD P. TEMPLE**
1803 Beverly Drive
Los Angeles, CA 90024
(310) 555-4167

## EMPLOYMENT

**Home Products, Los Angeles, CA**
**1994–present**
**Group Controller**

Manage a department of 40 people for a $900 million sales operating group within a high-technology national manufacturer of flexible packaging materials.

Responsibilities:

• Oversee the finance and accounting departments; responsibilities include reporting, ledgers, internal controls, payables, receivables, job costing, and standard costs.

• Annual and strategic planning, forecasting, and budgeting.

• MIS support and development for 15 manufacturing facilities and five regional sales offices.

Achievements:

• Implemented job costing systems and standardized financial reporting and accounting procedures.

• Consolidated divisional financial functions into one group.

• Completed a $75 million acquisition of a company and integrated its operations into the group.

**Royal Company, Inc., Los Angeles, CA**
**1990–1994**
**Assistant Corporate Controller**

Directed corporate department of 30 people for a home products company with $4 billion in sales.

Responsibilities:

• Finance, which included SEC reporting, registration statements, and shareholder reporting.

• General accounting, payroll, and fixed property accounting.

• Financial and capital planning, budgeting, forecasting, and analysis.

*Ronald P. Temple—page one of two*

Achievements:

- Involved in a major corporate restructuring.

- Installed new procedures, computer systems, and microcomputers.

- Simplified and automated administrative and accounting procedures.

**Royal Company, Inc., Los Angeles, CA**
**1986–1990**
**Financial Manager**

Managed a divisional financial function of five people for a high-technology manufacturing division.

Responsibilities:

- General accounting, financial reporting, systems development, and accounts receivable management.

- Investment analysis, budgeting, financial planning, and forecasting.

- Product line, geographic, and market segment reporting for sales and marketing functions.

Achievements:

- Installed computer systems covering order entry, production planning, invoicing, warehousing, and shipping functions.

**Maxwell House, Corporate Controller, 1984–1986**

**Royal Company, Inc., Financial Reporting Supervisor, 1982–1984**

**Louis, Montgomery, Sutro, CPAs, Staff Auditor, 1979–1980**

**California Settling Co., General Accountant, 1978–1979**

## EDUCATION

University of Southern California, Los Angeles, CA
M.B.A., Business Management, 1982

California State University, Long Beach
B.A., Accounting, 1978

*Ronald P. Temple—page two of two*

# K. ARTHUR LEWIS

*130 Tenth Street*
*Minneowa, MN 55494*
*home: (612) 555-8200*
*cell: (651) 555-7943*

## EDUCATION

Bachelor of Science degree in Economics, University of Nebraska, 1975

## WORK HISTORY

MANAGEMENT CONSULTANT, K. Arthur Lewis & Co., Minneapolis, MN
1994–present
Provide executive management services to financially troubled medium-sized firms. Review corporate strategies, operations, marketing, management information systems, banking relations, cash flow management, and personnel.

VICE PRESIDENT, FINANCE, Minnesota Engineers, St. Paul, MN
1986–1993
Responsible for all corporate financial control, treasury, and employee benefits functions in a company with revenues of $2 billion and 6,000 employees. Also directed Telecommunications and Management Information Systems administrative functions. Negotiated international contracts with complex tax and foreign exchange considerations. Developed a risk and cost containment strategy for foreign subsidiaries, increasing corporate operation results by $10 million. Installed advanced computer and telecommunications systems.

CONTROLLER, International Construction Group, Omaha, NE
1980–1986
Managed all financial activities as well as administrative control of support services. Directed staff of 150.

FINANCIAL AND ADMINISTRATIVE POSITIONS, Price Waterhouse, Omaha, NE
1975–1980
Performed financial services and managed financially troubled companies in construction, food processing, rail, and oil industries.

*K. Arthur Lewis—page one of two*

# RECENT ASSIGNMENTS—K. ARTHUR LEWIS & CO.

FENTON DOOR COMPANY, Minneapolis, MN
1999–2000
Manufacturer and distributor of door hardware for commercial and industrial buildings.

Improved operating effectiveness; expanded sales staffing and development; sold and relocated certain plant facilities; revised management and operating policies; reduced operating costs.

COLLINS GROUP, Minneapolis, MN
1997–present
Family-owned group of banking, real estate, and manufacturing companies.

Providing consulting services for potential investments, organizational restructure, and negotiation of contracts.

BLOOMINGTON CONCRETE COMPANY, Bloomington, MN
1996–present
Group of four companies involved in ready-mix operations and in cement transportation.

Disposed of a portion of the company, restructured operations, and implemented Chapter 11 reorganization plan. The company became profitable 15 months later.

Providing continued consulting advice for ongoing operations.

MIDWESTERN LEASING COMPANY, Edina, MN
1996–present
Lessor of equipment to the agricultural industry.

Reduced size of company's operations; sold marketable properties and equipment; managed non-marketable properties and equipment; collected lease payments. Currently in the process of liquidating the company.

**GERALD T. MASON**

48 Whispering Trees Lane
Oak Park, IL 60302
(312) 555-5268 home
(847) 555-9090 cell

**Objective:** A financial executive position in a moderately sized service business where streamlined systems and operations are key ingredients to corporate success.

**Summary:** Over 20 years of experience managing finance, operations, marketing, and administration functions. A business generalist skilled at discovering effective and economic solutions to increase earnings.

## ACCOMPLISHMENTS

**Finance:** Served as senior lending officer to accounts that included Dayton Hudson, Illinois Bell, AMAX Coal, Bank of Illinois, and Northwestern. Achieved bank profitability for the first time in three years.

**Operations:** Reduced operating expenses $100,000 a month over a twelve-month period. Developed productivity improvement programs that resulted in significant cost savings.

**Administration:** Directed over 250 people.
Managed human resources, computer operations, and marketing functions. Implemented new telecommunications system.

## EXPERIENCE

1999–present         MORGAN CONSULTING.         Oak Park, IL
Senior Associate: Consultant in financial controls, operations, and systems.

1998–1999         MICHIGAN LEASING.         Skokie, IL
Sales Broker: Brokered equipment leases from $10,000–$1,000,000.

1997–1998         PILGRIM FUNDS, INC.         Indianapolis, IN
Chief Operations Officer: Managed human resources, computer operations, and marketing functions. Reduced operating expenses $30,000 per month over a twelve-month period.

1993–1997         ILLINOIS NATIONAL BANK.         Peoria, IL
Chief Executive Officer: Achieved bank profitability for the first time in three years. Directed marketing, finance, and credit administration.

*page one of two*

1988–1993          HARBOR COMMERCIAL FUNDS.   Detroit, MI
Executive Vice President: Managed growth from $100 million to $400 million in four years. Developed productivity improvement programs that resulted in significant cost savings.

1982–1988          FIDELITY BANK.                    Chicago, IL
Vice President: Commercial lending officer to major accounts in Minneapolis, Indianapolis, and Illinois. Managed over $150 million in loans and $90 million in deposits.

1979–1982          STODDARD WOOD PRODUCTS.   Milwaukee, WI
Sales Manager, Midwestern Region

1976–1979          RAILROADMEN'S BANK.            Milwaukee, WI
Branch Manager

## EDUCATION

B.A., Business, University of Iowa, Iowa City, IA, 1974
M.B.A., Kellogg Graduate School of Management, Northwestern University, Evanston, IL, 1976

## ACTIVITIES

Oak Park Noon Rotary Club
Oak Park Chamber of Commerce
Chicago Boys and Girls Clubs

## Anna Nomura
### 335 Lake of the Isles Lane
### Minnetka, Minnesota 55673
### (612) 555-9090 home
### (612) 555-5476 work
### (651) 555-3434 cell

## EDUCATION

Mills College, Oakland, California
Degree: Bachelor of Science in Biology, minor in Economics
Graduate May 2001

Additional Study at University of Minnesota, Duluth
Center for Great Lakes Environmental Research,
Summer 1999

## EXPERIENCE

*Financial Intern*—Bank of America, San Francisco, California
Summer 2000

- Solved individual account problems for clients.

- Processed transfer of new stock for over 1000 client accounts after acquisition of Western Mutual Savings and Loan.

- Standardized management reports for customer service department.

*Environmental Law Intern*—Hanley and Moor Law Firm, St. Paul, Minnesota
Summer 1999

- Assisted in the preparation of pretrial files for clients in the environmental sector.

- Performed receptionist duties for busy front office while lead secretary was on six weeks' medical leave.

- Responsible for creation of firm's first website.

*Counselor*—Camp Castaway, Emery, Wisconsin
Summer 1998

- Instructed campers in scuba diving, snorkeling, lifesaving, and canoeing.

- Responsible for all campers between ages 13 and 18.

- Organized and coordinated group activities.

## SKILLS AND ACTIVITIES

Secretary, Environmental Action Club, Mills College.
Member, Neighborhood Improvement Association, Oakland, California.
Proficient in library research, writing, and editing.
Experienced in website design and management.

### DAWN CLARE SWITZER

**138 LONDON DRIVE
NEW HAVEN, CT 06520
(203) 555-5717 CELLULAR PHONE**

*OBJECTIVE*

Staff position as a tax accountant.

*PROFESSIONAL EXPERIENCE*

**Tax Staff Accountant.** 7/97 to present.
Coopers & Lybrand, New Haven, CT.

**Accountant/Bookkeeper.** 7/96 to 12/96.
Traditional Clothing, New Haven, CT.
Established and maintained accounts receivable, accounts payable, payroll, and inventory control.

**Waitress.** 4/95 to 12/96.
George's Restaurant, New Haven, CT.

**Office Assistant.** Summer 1996.
Tudor School, Hartford, CT.
Received and posted tuition payments. Maintained inventory and ordered school's food and supplies.

*EDUCATION*

B.S., Accounting, May 1997.
Southern Connecticut University, New Haven, CT.

*SKILLS AND CERTIFICATION*

CPA. Passed examination with highest honors.
Tax research and return preparation.
Proficient in Microsoft Excel.
Completed Coopers & Lybrand tax staff training program.

*REFERENCES*

Furnished on request.

## *Dora Vang*
*4891 Ravenna Blvd., #12*
*Seattle, WA 98185*
*(206) 555-4610*

## WORK EXPERIENCE

*RAINIER BANK,* 1994–present.

Began as commercial teller and advanced to personal banker. Responsible for opening new accounts, processing IRA accounts, handling certificates of deposit, and providing banking advice to customers.

*SEATTLE SAVINGS BANK,* 1992–1994.

Paying and receiving clerk. My responsibilities included bookkeeping, handling certificates of deposit, and assisting customers in balancing their accounts. Telemarketed bank services.

*BANK OF WASHINGTON,* 1987–1992.

Began as paying and receiving clerk and moved to safe deposit clerk. My duties included readying cash drawers and assisting customers in balancing their accounts. As safe deposit clerk, I led customers to their boxes and verified signatures as well as prepared rental statements and posted payments.

*BANK OF CANADA,* 1986–1987.

New accounts clerk. Responsible for opening new accounts, opening and closing certificates of deposit, and acting as branch receptionist.

## EDUCATION

University of British Columbia, Vancouver.
Graduated in 1995 with a degree in History and a minor in Accounting.

## REFERENCES

Furnished on request.

**HARRY GREENE**

**120 Crest Drive, #7E**
**Salt Lake City, UT 84112**
**(801) 555-5867 home**
**(801) 555-7690 cell**

**Work Experience:**

August 1997 to present
**Carl M. Haas & Co.,** Salt Lake City, UT
*Senior Auditor*
In charge of audit teams for clients in manufacturing, wholesale distributing, and retail sales. Prepare tax returns for individuals, corporations, and partnerships.
Perform general accounting services which include financial statement preparation.

March 1992 to May 1997
**Campus Camera,** Provo, UT
*Office Assistant*
Processed accounts receivable and computed job cost and profitability. Produced period-end production reports.

May 1996 to May 1997
**Brigham Young University,** Provo, UT
*Central Processing Clerk*
Processed student loans and performed general clerical duties for the Division of Financial Aid.

**Education:**

Brigham Young University, Provo, UT
Bachelor of Science in Accounting, 1997
Major GPA: 3.8, Overall GPA: 3.5

**Coursework:**

Auditing, Financial Accounting, Financial Management, Business Communications, and Computer Science.

**Activities:**

National Association of Accountants, Utah Chapter
Vice President of Beta Alpha Psi, National Accounting Honorary Society

## LAWRENCE K. MCNAMARA

6445 Graham Road                                    (303) 555-7820 (home)
Englewood, CO 80111                                 (303) 555-9889 (work)

### EXPERIENCE

**Price Waterhouse & Co.,** Denver, CO
Tax Manager
1995 to present

*Responsibilities:*
Taxation consultation, research, and compliance for clients.
Supervision, training, and evaluation of professional staff.
New business development.
Instructor of national tax courses and seminars.
Hiring of tax department professional staff.

**Arthur Andersen & Co.,** Colorado Springs, CO
Senior Tax Manager and Director of Tax Recruiting
1988 to 1995

**Arthur Andersen & Co., Colorado Springs, CO**
Tax Intern
Spring 1988

**Deloitte & Touche,** Denver, CO
Audit Intern
Summer 1987

### EDUCATION AND TRAINING

University of Colorado at Boulder
M.B.A., Business Taxation, 1997
GPA: 3.8

University of Colorado at Boulder
B.S., Business Administration, Accounting, 1988
GPA: 3.7

Price Waterhouse & Co.
National and local courses in taxation, management, and recruiting, 1995 to present

Arthur Andersen & Co.
National and local courses in taxation, auditing, management, and recruiting, 1988 to 1995

*Lawrence K. McNamara—page one of two*

## HONORS AND ACHIEVEMENTS

*Professional:*
American Institute of Certified Public Accountants
Colorado Society of Certified Public Accountants
Passed CPA exam on first attempt, May 1988

*School:*
Beta Alpha Psi (honorary accounting fraternity)
Dean's list
Colorado Buffalos Associate (official hosts of University of Colorado)

*Civic:*
Goodwill Industries, Board of Directors
University of Colorado, Board of Directors

## INTERESTS

Bicycling, golf, and mountain climbing

**EVAN P. GRIFFEY**

**40 Pine Mountain Court**
**Greenville, South Carolina 29613**
**(803) 555-8307 home phone**
**(803) 555-3478 cell phone**

## EDUCATION

WHARTON BUSINESS SCHOOL, Philadelphia, PA
Master of Business Administration, 1986

CARLETON COLLEGE, Northfield, MN
Bachelor of Arts in Economics, 1985

## EXPERIENCE

WOODLAND FURNISHINGS, Greenville, SC
**Vice President of Finance,** 1998–present. Established financial and administrative systems and controls and developed recapitalization plan.

ALLIED PARTNERS, Charleston, SC
**Senior Vice President of Corporate Finance,** 1996–1998. Responsible for financial planning, accounting, financial analysis, and management reporting for all Allied companies.

**Senior Vice President of Portfolio Finance,** 1995–1996. Responsible for accounting and reporting on the firm's 90 real estate investments, which included the acquisition, management, and disposition of properties.

**Vice President of Finance,** 1991–1995. Responsible for accounting and reporting, corporate planning, budgeting, cash management, and administration of the office building investment division.

WILLIAM G. ESTES, Charleston, SC
**Vice President of Finance,** 1991. Responsible for accounting, financial analysis, corporate planning, and budgeting for residential mortgage loans.

FOWLER CORPORATION, Charlotte, NC
**Controller,** 1988–1991. Responsible for accounting, financial planning, and management reporting for 400-employee publication firm.

**Assistant to the Corporate Controller,** 1986–1988. Analyzed corporate strategic alternatives. Conducted operational review of financial controls, cost systems, and management information systems.

**CARL G. HENDERSON**
**2598 Peach Boulevard**
**Atlanta, GA 30332**
**(404) 555-1298**

## EXPERIENCE:

8/96 to present
**Assistant Vice President/Credit Officer**
Commerce Bank Georgia, Atlanta, GA

Obtain credit and financial information necessary to assess the financial risk in commercial and installment loans. Analyze the information, draft loan reports, and make appropriate recommendations. Interview loan applicants to determine credit qualifications and borrowing needs. Provide deposit and loan services to existing customers. Prepare monthly problem loan reports.

4/84 to 7/96
**Assistant Vice President/Loan Administration**
First National Bank, Atlanta, GA

Directed the preparation of commercial, consumer, real estate, and construction loan documentation. Assisted the senior credit officer in supervising loan compliance and regulatory issues applicable to bank lending. Wrote material governing lending practices, policies, and procedures. Exercised approval authority within established limits of $50,000 to individuals and $100,000 to businesses. Provided collection assistance for commercial, consumer, and real estate problem loans.

1/82 to 4/84
**Assistant Bank Examiner**
Regional Banks, Atlanta, GA

Assisted in bank examinations and loan audits. Reviewed and analyzed problem loans.

5/81 to 10/82
**Loan Officer**
Commerce Bank Georgia, Atlanta, GA

Interviewed loan applicants, analyzed their requests, and made appropriate recommendations.

4/75 to 5/81
**Credit Officer**
Atlanta National Bank, Marietta, GA

Directed credit department functions.

## EDUCATION:

B.A., Business Administration, Emory University

## COMMUNITY:

Insurance Committee, Atlanta Chamber of Commerce
Board of Directors, Bankers Club of Georgia

*ELI LEVINSON*
*908 Jefferson Heights, #6B*
*Minneapolis, MN 55404*
*(612) 555-1298 home*
*(651) 555-3764 cell*

## OBJECTIVE

To secure a midlevel management position in finance that will utilize my analytical, managerial, and training skills.

## SUMMARY

A proven self-starter with exceptional communication and interpersonal skills. Extensive management experience in diverse fields including financial services, data processing, field operations, and manufacturing.

## ACCOMPLISHMENTS

Coordinated data processing operations for the 2000 census in the Minneapolis office, included training supervisors and staff members.

Served as technical advisor on operational activities of the data processing and field departments during the 2000 census.

Coordinated field activities of over 800 employees in conducting a complete enumeration of population and housing in the state; included managing the preparation, check-in, and review of census materials.

Managed departmental budget.

Developed compliance, financial, and operations procedures for full-service brokerage house.

Reconciled conversion of customer accounts between clearing firms.

Taught securities training classes to prospective stock brokers.

Implemented financial procedures for securities firm for reconciliations and financial reporting.

Streamlined commission accounting procedures.

*Eli Levinson, page one of two*

## CAREER HISTORY

U.S. DEPARTMENT OF COMMERCE—BUREAU OF THE CENSUS
Minneapolis, MN
1997–2000
Manager, Field and EDP Operations

VENTURE CAPITAL CORPORATION
Baltimore, MD
1995–1997
Vice President, Chief Financial Officer, Chief Compliance Officer

KEN FOX AND ASSOCIATES
Madison, WI
1994–1995
Chief Financial Officer

MIDWESTERN CAPITAL SECURITIES, INC.
Madison, WI
1992–1994
Securities Analyst

NORTHERN FINANCIAL SERVICES
Pittsburgh, PA
1990–1992
Supervisor of Compliance, Supervisor of Operations

NEW YORK STOCK EXCHANGE
New York, NY
1987–1989
Lead Clerk, Options Department

## PROFESSIONAL LICENSES

Foreign Currency Options Principal, 1995
Debt Registered Options Principal, 1995
Financial and Operations Principal, 1992
Municipal Securities Principal, 1992
Registered Options Principal, 1990

## EDUCATION

University of Pennsylvania, B.A., 1987

**FRANK HOWARD**
5643 Cherry Lane
Richmond, VA 23230
(804) 555-9658

## OBJECTIVE

A position in accounting that utilizes my experience and training and offers an opportunity for professional growth.

## SKILLS

Microsoft Excel
Microsoft Word
Excellent written and oral communications
Computer accounting program development

## WORK EXPERIENCE

4/97 - present
ASSISTANT VICE PRESIDENT
Bank of Virginia, Richmond, VA

- Prepare monthly financial management reports as well as the Federal Reserve reports.

- Balance monthly general ledger accounts.

- Direct payroll, personnel, and insurance functions.

- Purchase and distribute office supplies.

- Supervise account investments and reconcilements.

11/94 - 4/97
PAYROLL & ACCOUNTS PAYABLE ASSISTANT
Jefferson Medical Center, Richmond, VA

9/90 - 10/94
BOOKKEEPER & TELLER
Dominion Bank, Richmond, VA

## EDUCATION

Virginia Commonwealth University, B.S., Accounting, 1990

*References furnished upon request.*

## Russell P. Arnerich

*4156 Beach Road*
*Providence, RI 02912*
*(401) 555-6361 cellular*
*(401) 555-3334 home*

**Objective:** To obtain a financial research position with a major commercial bank.

### Education

1999 – 2001 New York University Business School, M.B.A., Finance

1993 – 1997 Brown University, B.S., Industrial Engineering

Honors: Dean's list, Brown Foundation Scholarship for study in Europe

### Experience

**Consultant, Center for Risk Management,** Providence, RI - Summer 2000

Developed financial models for cost structure and economic impact of various Rhode Island health care reform scenarios. Designed analytic approach.

**Assistant Product Manager, Quality Software,** Cambridge, MA - 1998 to 1999

Participated in the release of a foreign language tutorial program. Involved in providing technical support, writing magazine ads and press releases, and processing invoices.

**English Instructor, Sorbonne Language Center,** Paris, France - 1997 to 1998

Taught conversational English to French executives and engineers.

**Intern, National Assembly,** Paris, France - Summer 1997

Analyzed and researched pertinent issues. Wrote correspondence to constituents.

### Additional Information

Foreign Language: French
Website design and programming

# *Sample Cover Letters*

March 27, 20--

RICHARD ADAMS
145 Eden Glen Drive
Cincinnati, Ohio 45228
(513) 555-5071

Mr. Clark Long, President
International Foods, Inc.
80 State Street
Chicago, IL 60641

Dear Mr. Long:

I am interested in applying for the position of Corporate Treasurer at International Foods, Inc. Bob Clinton of Quaker Oats told me about this opening and suggested that I contact you.

Currently, I am Treasurer of Morgan Frozen Foods in Cincinnati. My knowledge of the foods industry is extensive; I have also been a brand assistant at General Foods.

I will call you next week to follow up on this letter and to find out about the possibility of interviewing for the position of Corporate Treasurer.

Sincerely,

Richard Adams

July 24, 20--

310 East 80th Street, #201
New York, NY 10028

Mr. Charles Dixon
Morgan Stanley
60 Broad Street
New York, NY 10010

Dear Mr. Dixon:

I would like to be considered for the position of Financial Analyst at Morgan Stanley. I strongly believe the investment banking industry is an area in which my academic accomplishments and personal qualities would be an asset.

At Cornell University, I have explored a diverse academic program while pursuing a main focus in business. Coursework in the fields of economics and statistics has allowed me to develop the research and quantitative skills that will enable me to quickly become proficient at performing various financial analyses. Moreover, my experiences in past employment and my extracurricular activities have served to enhance my competence in the areas of interpersonal communication and business interaction.

Morgan Stanley has attracted my attention by virtue of its size and reputation in the field of investment banking. The opportunity to learn from the top professionals is invaluable.

Thank you very much for your time and consideration. I can best be reached by cell phone at 567-555-8989 or by E-mail at speterson@xxx.net. I hope to have the opportunity to talk with you in the near future.

Yours truly,

Samuel Peterson

December 28, 20--

Kate J. Romerhaus
82 Elm Street
Ann Arbor, MI 48109

Mr. Andrew Finney
Director of Human Resources
The Radisson Hotel
6000 Ford Boulevard
Ann Arbor, MI 48120

Dear Mr. Finney:

I am writing to inquire about any openings you may have for a bookkeeper. My experience in bookkeeping includes working for Dayton Hudson, a major department store, and Applebee's restaurant chain.

I have strong computer skills on both IBM and Macintosh systems and am proficient in database and accounting programs. Furthermore, I am willing to work flexible hours.

If you have an interest in further discussing my qualifications, please contact me at (313) 555-9427.

Sincerely,

Kate J. Romerhaus

April 2, 20--

Laura K. Manning
473 Hill Drive West
Kenosha, WI 53143
(414) 555-6320

Ms. Alice Oliver
Human Resources Director
Dean Witter
1 Witter Center
Milwaukee, WI 53226

Dear Ms. Oliver:

I will be graduating from the University of Wisconsin in May 2001. I am seeking a position as an institutional broker.

My education at the University of Wisconsin has prepared me well to contribute to your organization. My quantitative skills have been sharpened by coursework in statistics and calculus. I have also taken a wide range of courses in such subjects as economics, logic, and philosophy, which have helped me to improve my ability to think analytically. In addition, my decision to graduate one year early indicates my high level of motivation.

I have had some work experiences that would help me be a valuable asset to your organization. Last summer, I was an intern at Merrill Lynch where I received firsthand exposure to the workings of a large institutional sales firm. The previous summer, I worked for a small brokerage house in Kenosha. I have passed the Series 7 exams and am now studying for the Series 3 exams.

I should like to meet with you and demonstrate that I have the qualifications and the personality that make for a successful broker. Many thanks for your time and consideration.

Sincerely,

Laura K. Manning

Enclosure

**DAWN CLARE SWITZER**
**138 LONDON DRIVE**
**NEW HAVEN, CT 06520**
**(203) 555-5717 CELLULAR PHONE**

June 15, 20--

Ms. Louise Sterling
Peat Marwick
300 East 46th Street
New York, NY 10020

Dear Ms. Sterling:

I am writing to inquire about any openings your firm may have for Tax Staff Accountants.

My experience in accounting includes working as an Accountant/Bookkeeper for the past five years. Recently, I passed the CPA examination and received highest honors.

Working at Peat Marwick would be a unique and challenging experience. The company has attracted my attention by virtue of its size and reputation in the field of accounting firms. I am very appreciative of your time and consideration.

Sincerely,

Dawn Clare Switzer

Rural Route One, Box 229
Dalton, WI 53926
Telephone: (920) 555-4396

November 19, 20--

Ms. Cynthia Parker
State Street Bank
46 Revere Boulevard
Boston, MA 02117

Dear Ms. Parker:

As you requested in our recent conversation, I am sending you a copy of my resume. My goal is to find a senior management position in banking in which I can expand my experience in international banking.

My background includes fluency in French, along with an understanding of the French culture and lifestyle. My strong banking experience covers foreign exchange, international money transfers, interest rate swaps, and letters of credit.

I am confident that my background and career goals can benefit your organization in many ways. Please contact me so that we can discuss my experience and your needs in the detail they both deserve.

Sincerely,


Leta M. Von der Sump

Enclosure

August 17, 20--

Ms. Martha Osborne
Bank of America
555 California Street
San Francisco, CA 94104

Dear Ms. Osborne:

On the advice of David Fong of Bank of Hawaii, I am submitting the enclosed resume for your consideration. I have over 20 years of experience in all fields of banking, including operations, lending, and business development. Currently, I am seeking a position that provides me with the opportunity to use and enhance my extensive skills. I would be pleased to find this position at Bank of America.

I am a strong self-starter with proven abilities to meet and exceed challenging objectives, and I am very experienced with banking practices in the Far East and Pacific Basin. I am currently an Assistant Vice President and Branch Manager at Bank of Hawaii in Honolulu.

Please contact me at your convenience to discuss our mutual interests. I can be reached by cell phone at (808) 555-9876, or at home at (808) 555-7834. I look forward to hearing from you soon.

Sincerely,

Rachel Anderson
34 Diamond Head Way
Honolulu, HI 96813

*February 9, 20--*

**CARLOS RODRIGUEZ**
*68 Via Robles Drive*
*Valencia, CA 91355*
*(805) 555-6050 home*
*(805) 555-9900 cellular*

Mr. Nick Ponti, President
Community Bank of Coral Gables
200 Main Street
Coral Gables, FL 33124

Dear Mr. Ponti:

Are you getting the maximum results possible from your commercial lending activities? Have you penetrated the sought-after middle market? If not, my background may be of interest to you.

My extensive commercial lending experience includes exposure in credit analysis, investments, and planning. I am particularly skilled at developing and retaining customer relations through innovative and professional service.

During the past 25 years, I have held management positions of increasing responsibility covering all aspects of commercial lending. As an analytical and enthusiastic problem solver, I can provide your bank with the experience necessary to achieve an improved bottom line.

The following are a few of my major accomplishments that may interest your organization:

• Established a $40 million industrial and commercial loan portfolio that achieved consistent returns.

• Designed new security and foreign exchange trading activities.

• Assisted a major Japanese bank in opening operations in California.

• Produced a 25 percent return on equity with the "account officer" concept.

I have earned a B.A. in Economics from the University of Madrid, Spain. I speak fluent Spanish, which should be an asset in Coral Gables. I am sure that I could make the kind of forward-thinking, growth-oriented contributions your bank would require. I have only presented a brief summary of my qualifications and accomplishments and therefore would like to meet with you to discuss ways in which my extensive background could make a major contribution to your bank.

Sincerely,

Carlos Rodriguez

MARTIN CHANG
964 NORTH TENTH STREET
SPRINGFIELD, IL 62713
(217) 555-5240


October 16, 20--


Mr. Jeff Franklin
Human Resources
Bethlehem Steel
4000 Hammond Road
Gary, IN 46634


Dear Mr. Franklin:

I would greatly appreciate the opportunity to talk to you about your firm's need for a financial analyst. The position you advertised in the Chicago Tribune on October 14 interests me because it would enable me to utilize my analytical skills in the heavy industry sector.

My education and work experiences have certainly prepared me to contribute to Bethlehem Steel. My coursework in economics and my position as senior financial analyst with the Illinois Department of Commerce have honed my quantitative and analytical skills. Furthermore, I am well acquainted with the steel industry as I have represented the State of Illinois in its economic development efforts targeted toward the steel industry. I am confident that these qualifications will be assets in a position as a financial analyst with your firm.

I appreciate your time and consideration. I hope to have a chance to talk to you about the advertised position.

Sincerely,



Martin Chang
Enclosure: Resume

February 9, 20--

Lydia Parsons
3306 Metro Square
Tacoma, WA 98416

Dear Ms. Parsons:

Thank you for talking with me on February 8 about the personal banker position at Columbia Bank. After our conversation, I find that I am very interested in the position. I am impressed with the emphasis that Columbia Bank places on customer satisfaction, as it has always been my number one priority. With my solid experience as a personal banker, I believe that I would be an asset to the Columbia Bank.

Thank you for your time and consideration. I hope to hear from you soon.

Sincerely,

*Dora Vang*
*4891 Ravenna Boulevard, #12*
*Seattle, WA 98185*
*(206) 555-4610*

September 12, 20--

1000 Chestnut Street
San Francisco, CA 94117
415/555-9080

Human Resources Manager
John P. Browne & Company
400 Market Street
San Francisco, CA 94103

To Whom It May Concern:

After five years in public accounting with Coopers & Lybrand, I am exploring new career opportunities. I am especially interested in working at a midsize accounting firm where I can have increased contact with clients.

During my years at Coopers & Lybrand, I have obtained expertise in auditing, budgeting, preparing reports, and supervising senior and staff accountants. I am seeking a position in the San Francisco area that would allow me to continue to develop my skills as part of a small financial management team.

Enclosed is my resume for your review. I look forward to meeting with you to discuss your organization and the possibility of our affiliation.

Sincerely,


Grace Delaney
Enclosure

# MARGARET FONG

*16201 Blossom Hill Road*
*San Jose, CA 95008*
*(408) 555-2985*

December 19, 20--

Mr. J. D. Saunders
The Bank of Providence
500 East Market Street
Providence, RI 02903

Dear Mr. Saunders:

In today's fast-changing banking arena, adaptability and a goal-oriented attitude are among the most valuable prerequisites a successful bank executive must have to survive and prosper. I have demonstrated these qualities as a Regional and Branch Manager for the Community Bank of Los Gatos in California.

I am an experienced financial lending professional with strong analytical skills in all areas of banking. My background includes commercial and construction lending, management, and new business development. As Regional Manager, I have organized a new construction lending department and improved the credit quality of a substandard loan portfolio.

As I am resettling on the East Coast, I am now looking for a new banking position as a Regional Manager. I have read about the innovative lending practices of your bank in American Banker and have been intrigued with your imaginative solutions to common lending problems.

I believe I can make a valuable contribution to the continued development of The Bank of Providence. I would very much like to meet with you to describe the work I have done in implementing new lending procedures. Please contact me at the above number at your earliest convenience.

Sincerely,

Margaret Fong

April 14, 20--

Mr. Nathaniel Comfort
Bank of California
255 Grand Avenue
Los Angeles, CA 90017

Dear Mr. Comfort:

I am sending you my resume at the suggestion of Caroline Martin. Caroline was my former colleague at The State Bank of Phoenix. My previous job there was eliminated in January 2001 as the result of a corporate takeover. I am seeking a position as part of an executive management team that can use my expertise for the enhancement of the organization.

I have a diverse background with banks in metropolitan areas in credit and loan support functions. I also have experience in managing daily bank operations.

If you have an interest in contacting me, please call me at (602) 555-2311.

I look forward to hearing from you soon.

Sincerely,


Arthur K. Montgomery
614 Camelback Road
Phoenix, AZ 85021

### Carol J. Fowler
**3004 79th Street**
**Philadelphia, PA 19107**
**(215) 555-9218 home**
**(215) 555-0878 cellular**

June 21, 20--

First National Bank of Pennsylvania
120 First Street North
Philadelphia, PA 19101

To Whom It May Concern:

I read with interest the First National Bank of Pennsylvania's advertisement in the Philadelphia Inquirer for a customer service representative.

I have worked in customer service, the merchant window, safe deposit, and general branch management. During each of the last three years, I have received "Teller of the Week" awards. I have also been chosen to attend sales rallies as the branch representative.

My experience in the banking environment has shown that I can work well with people. Besides having considerable skills as a teller, I have been told that my communications skills are excellent.

I am available to meet with a representative of the First National Bank of Pennsylvania at his or her convenience.

Thank you for your consideration.

Sincerely,


Carol J. Fowler

March 13, 20--

Jackson J. Paige
4919 Lake Shore Drive
Chicago, IL 60604
(312) 555-4681

Walter G. Needham
Bankers Trust
130 Liberty Street
New York, NY 10015

Dear Mr. Needham:

I would be very interested in talking with you about a career at Bankers Trust, specifically as a financial analyst in the real estate department.

At DePaul University, I am majoring in economics, which gives me the analytical skills needed for the position. Furthermore, I have taken classes that emphasize the role of technology in the investment world.

I have considerable practical experience to reinforce my strong academic record including meaningful internships during the two past summers. At First Bank of Chicago, I was a commercial loan coordinator, which gave me firsthand knowledge of real estate. At the Star Bank in Chicago, I was involved in the back-office operations in the international banking department.

Thank you for your consideration.

Yours truly,


Jackson J. Paige

**120 Crest Drive, #7E**
**Salt Lake City, UT 84112**
**801/555-5867 home**
**801/555-7690 cellular**

January 20, 20--

Coopers & Lybrand
Branch Manager
Merchant's Bank Building
Suite 608
Indianapolis, IN 46206

To Whom It May Concern:

I wish to apply for a position as a senior auditor. I hold a bachelor's degree in accounting and was awarded an Elijah Watt Sells Gold Award for receiving the highest grades in passing all four sections of the CPA examination at one time.

My high level of achievement on the CPA examination as well as three years of successful experience as an auditor in charge of audit teams for Fortune 500 clients indicate my mastery of the intricacies of accounting. I work effectively under pressure and handle my time efficiently. With this background, I am confident that I would be an asset to Coopers & Lybrand.

Enclosed is a copy of my resume for your review. I would greatly appreciate the opportunity to discuss my qualifications with you.

Thank you for your consideration.

Sincerely,

Harry Greene

October 7, 20--

**806 El Pintado Road**
**San Antonio, TX 78284**
**(512) 555-4934**
**(512) 555-9098 cellular**

Mr. John Courier
The San Antonio Construction Company
P.O. Box 357
San Antonio, TX 78290

Dear Mr. Courier:

Please accept this letter as an application for the position of controller of the San Antonio Construction Company. I have enclosed a copy of my resume for your review.

During my present employment as a group controller for the National Oil Company in San Antonio, I have developed strategic, annual, and capital plans as well as accounting policies and procedures. My formal education includes a B.S. in accounting with a minor in industries engineering. I also hold a CPA license in Texas. Furthermore, I possess the people management skills that the position of controller requires.

I would like very much to discuss my qualifications in an interview.

Sincerely,

Kenneth H. Allen

## JANET K. LEVANS

### 460 WASHINGTON COURT
### PHILADELPHIA, PA 19130
### (215) 555-8958

May 3, 20--

Brooks Financial Consulting Co.
1029 Century Park East, Suite 1000
Los Angeles, CA 90067

Greetings:

I am responding to your ad in the Wall Street Journal for an associate position. Through my work experience at Morgan Stanley, I have acquired a facility in quantitative and qualitative evaluation of structures for the sale or financing of trophy real estate assets. I have gained an understanding of the elements of transactions and various negotiating styles, managed and built client relationships, and worked with potential investors.

Recently, I received my M.B.A. degree from the Wharton School of Business. My graduate course work emphasized finance and accounting. As part of the Wharton M.B.A. program, I was involved in a strategic and marketing field study for a major entertainment company's investment in an E-commerce venture.

As requested, I am enclosing my resume and salary history. I look forward to discussing with you soon the career opportunities at Brooks Financial Consulting Company.

Sincerely,


Janet K. Levans

March 27, 20--

Mr. Colin Kennedy
Director of Human Resources
First Bank of California
683 Veda Boulevard
Los Angeles, CA 90010

Dear Mr. Kennedy:

I am seeking a challenging position that will give me the greatest possible exposure to the banking industry. My interest in banking is inspired by my work experience over the last two summers as a loan administrator at California Mortgage Insurance Company and as an analyst at Merrill Lynch.

Now looking to explore the "real world" after four years as an economics and history major at the University of Southern California, I see banking as the best way to utilize my talents effectively and to reach my career objectives. I am a highly motivated, high-energy person with strong interpersonal and group skills. As captain of the cross-country team, I have participated in numerous activities that require teamwork. I want to work for a firm where team spirit and peer support are ingredients as important for success as they were on the USC cross-country team, which won the conference championship last year.

Thank you for your time and for assessing my abilities to become part of your bank.

Sincerely,


John S. Kelsey
4689 Beach Street
La Jolla, CA 92093

### ERIC C. LAWTON

*24961 Erie Parkway*
*Cleveland, Ohio 44106*

January 11, 20--

Mr. Christopher Wylie
Peat Marwick
89 South First Street
Cleveland, Ohio 44109

Dear Christopher:

It was a pleasure talking with you on the phone on Monday, January 10th. I am currently in the process of expanding my financial services business, which specializes in the area of financial consulting for moderately sized companies. My main focus is on companies that have a need for an interim financial consultant in the capacity of Chief Financial Officer.

I have an extensive background in financial management. My last two positions were as Chief Financial Officer and Vice President of Finance/Controller of a $15 million computer equipment manufacturer and a $25 million automotive instrumentation company. My experience includes broad exposure in the areas of cost accounting and management information systems.

I am looking forward to talking with you in the near future. Any consideration you can offer me will be sincerely appreciated.

Yours truly,


Eric C. Lawton
(216) 555-4971 home
(216) 555-8976 cellular